Queering the Pulpit

Queering the Pulpit

A Sexegetical Approach to Preaching an Inclusive Word

KARYN L. WISEMAN

CASCADE *Books* · Eugene, Oregon

QUEERING THE PULPIT
A Sexegetical Approach to Preaching an Inclusive Word

Cascade Books
An Imprint of Wipf and Stock Publishers
199 W. 8th Ave., Suite 3
Eugene, OR 97401

www.wipfandstock.com

PAPERBACK ISBN: 978-1-6667-8198-4
HARDCOVER ISBN: 978-1-6667-8199-1
EBOOK ISBN: 978-1-6667-8200-4

Cataloguing-in-Publication data:

Names: Wiseman, Karyn L., author.

Title: Queering the pulpit : a sexegetical approach to preaching an inclusive word / Karyn L. Wiseman.

Description: Eugene, OR: Cascade Books, 2024 | Includes bibliographical references.

Identifiers: ISBN 978-1-6667-8198-4 (paperback) | ISBN 978-1-6667-8199-1 (hardcover) | ISBN 978-1-6667-8200-4 (ebook)

Subjects: LCSH: Preaching. | Queer theology. | Church and minorities.

Classification: BV4221 W60 2024 (paperback) | BV4221 (ebook)

VERSION NUMBER 110624

Contents

Acknowledgments | vii

An Introduction | 1

Chapter One
Telling My Story | 12

Chapter Two
A Brief History of Queer Lives in Context | 26

Chapter Three
Tackling the Clobber Passages | 48

Chapter Four
Can We Find a "Yes, PERIOD" Theology? | 65

Chapter Five
Sexegetical Sermon Crafting | 83

Chapter Six
Queering the Pulpit: A Case Study | 99

Bibliography | 111

Acknowledgments

I CANNOT EXPRESS ENOUGH my gratitude for the number of hands and voices that have helped birth this book. No one can do this work without a cloud of witnesses and laborers.

My story starts with my birth family, who have loved me my whole life. They haven't always been smooth relationships but over time we have come to understand and appreciate each other. As I state in the book, I hid my secret for years and continued to live under a carefully engineered shame and fear-lined closet. My parents, Nancy and Keith, have been the best parents and they know the stories I tell are from my perspective and they didn't know what I was going through much of the time because of that closet and my deep fear. My sisters, Karla and Kim, experienced only what I let them know about. I owe so much to these amazing members of my birth family. The continued love and support from all of them is the dearest gift.

My amazing wife, Cindy, and our son, Shelby, have stood by me in thick and thin. I could not possibly do this without them. I am so blessed by them both. I thank Cindy for the many—and I mean many—versions she proofread. Cindy, you make this life journey so much better than I ever thought I would experience. If I knew at sixteen what my life would be now, I wouldn't possibly believe it, but it's a reality. Love you, babe.

Two people essential to this book are my dear, dear friend and mentor, h. sharon howell, who was the one who heard the words, "I'm gay" for the first time when I was sixteen. My life might never have extended beyond high school or college without her encouragement, affirmation, and acceptance. Matt O'Rear has been a friend and colleague for fourteen years. He opened his heart to share his church's "Drag Me To Church" event to use as a case study. His collaboration and support have been so delightful.

I also want to thank the United Lutheran Seminary Gettysburg + Philadelphia administration, board, faculty, and staff for their support of my sabbatical year, out of which comes this book.

I thank Gloria Dei Church, where I served as lead pastor, who helped navigate my pastoral leadership needs and my sabbatical time for the writing of this book. Their gracious support and love allowed me to carve out writing time every week of this past year. Thank you.

My heart is full and I thank you all!

An Introduction

MANY QUEER PEOPLE HAVE endured sermons, lectures, therapy sessions, Sunday school lessons, Bible studies, and other uncomfortable situations where statements were proclaimed loudly and clearly that their identity, their sexuality, their body, their gender or gender expression, and their whole being is an affront to G_d,[1] that their love is immoral and even criminal, and that this abnormal and abhorrent behavior has been chosen by them as a "preference" over the presumed heteronormative behavior. I absolutely and unequivocally state that these beliefs are baseless lies told to make anti-gay heterosexual persons feel more comfortable and to continue an interpretation of the Bible and theology that is exclusive and damaging to Queer folx.[2] Deep conversations, reinterpretations of damaging texts, and more experience with the gay community in personal, religious, and social occasions has led to some expansive opportunities for deeper understanding between these two groups of people over the past years. However, there are still biblical interpretations and experiences in the church that need attention to create an atmosphere of affirmation, acceptance, and love—especially in pulpits and pastoral leadership. This is where this book is leading the reader, into an opportunity to understand

1. This way of designating G_d allows for the multiple ways we can know G_d. It shows a more open expression that expands on the language that I grew up with and beyond what I was taught about inclusive language in seminary.

2. Use of *folx* is an attempt to use language that is expansive and inclusive. I use it as a way to explore how the use of nonbinary or non-gendered words can help heal the wounds of the Queer community.

the lives, faith, and experiences of the Queer community in the church and beyond. I hope to create a new homiletical and hermeneutical process to preach from our pulpits and in physical, social, digital, public, and religious spaces and also in the world by thought and deed to affirm and address the exclusion of the Queer community from the church. Even understanding the language, phrases, and acronyms used can be problematic.

First, I want to unpack the word *Queer*. When I was a teenager, into my young adult life, and even into middle age, I heard the word *Queer* as a negative and hateful word used to name someone as deviant and abnormal. On many occasions, the word was directed at me, and it was painful. This negative language can make an impact on the emotional and psychological development of anyone who hears these words and others thrown in their direction. Hearing words like *faggot, queer, lesbo*, and other vile "name calling" directed at me led to a crisis I hid for years. I tried to fit in by wearing dresses in my first few churches and even wore a light application of makeup. And I was miserable. I brace when I enter public bathrooms wearing a hoodie, jeans, and a ballcap to be told I am in the wrong restroom, or when I am called "sir" by the waitstaff where we're dining. Those words hurt, too. I am not alone in enduring these experiences.

They are happening less frequently, I admit, but I still brace my body and my mind for the confrontation or the misgendering. It has made me feel uncomfortable, unloved, and damaged, and led to a significant amount of pain and shame. It has for a lot of my life. The damage and the self-loathing I felt were a heavy load that took years and a great therapist to come to a different place emotionally and mentally. I still struggle with some of it now as a sixty-one-year-old lesbian who struggled with the word *Queer*. The word has been reclaimed by many younger Queer folx in their defining and redefining of self as a bold and proud statement of identity and as a more expansive language for the community. It took time for me to come around to the usage of that term as a potential positive reframing of my identity. However, I am fully on the Queer pride train now. I use it in my social media presence and in my preaching and teaching. That was a huge learning curve for me. You will read it throughout the book. So be prepared if you need some personal discernment to understand the reframing that will come with this book for a moment. It celebrates the use of the word *Queer* that may or may or may not be part of your lexicon. Some of you may have to come to a moment of self-awareness to forgive yourself of your own use of the word as a weapon to defame and insult a gay person in your life or for using the word *Queer* toward anyone that looks "gay" or "Queer" to you. Seek that forgiveness in your own life and know that G_d loves you for who you are, not for who you might be. It's a phrase I use in all my classes at the seminary and beyond. Throughout this book you will be invited to learn something new about the task of Queering your preaching. You may find some of it evokes questions you need to work on for yourself, and reading this book will probably make it necessary to process your own feelings, but do the work and it will create in you a deeper awareness and understanding of the Queer community. It may be tough. It may also be emotional. I know I have cried a few times writing about events that still can cause me pain, but not like they have in the past. Be open to the transformation that is possible here for you and your people, because you can be the difference for so many.

Second, the alphabet of the Queer community that you see in use in discussions around identity is vast and varied. Growing up in the 1970s and eighties, I only heard of two identities outside of the heteronormative expectations—those were gay and lesbian. It was clear, if you were not heterosexual, you were either a gay man or a lesbian. That was the limit of my understanding of sexuality and gender, and it did not give any hint of the fluidity and expansiveness of the entire Queer community. Later the B for bisexual and the T for transgender became part of the defining acronym of gay life known at that time to be LGBT. It was all I knew. But I knew no one who identified as transgender until well into my thirties. The letter did not mean a lot to me. Now a more wholistic view of the complexities of sexuality, gender, gender expression, and identity has resulted in an important process of defining the

Queer community as broadly and as boldly as possible. There are so many options. One very expansive acronym is LGBTQQIP2SAA,[3] which stands for lesbian, gay, bisexual, transgender, queer, questioning, intersex, pansexual, two-spirit (2S), androgynous, and asexual. However, none of us are just one thing. We have multiple understandings of self and a lot of struggles to live into them.

> There are tons of identities that we either take up or are imposed on us: From plant-mom, houseless, or Lutheran to trans, Asian American, or a gay bear. Sometimes societies or institutions trap us in these—like when someone assigned female at birth comes out as a man, they're always haunted and confined by the "trans" that comes before "man." But at the same time, being trans links that person to a community, a diverse yet collective experience of other folks like them.[4]

I have offered a course called Race, Gender, Sexuality, and Leadership at each of the seminaries where I have taught. When I started that course, sixteen years ago at Hood Theological Seminary, in Salisbury, North Carolina, not one person in any of my courses expressed an interest in defining themselves other than by name, denomination, years of experience, and where they were from. I had never asked the pronoun or identity question in that course. I was closeted myself, so I taught that course in ways that were inauthentic to me. How do you teach about affirmation and acceptance of folx with nonbinary genders and who identify as Queer when you won't proclaim it yourself? It was not the first and would, unfortunately, not be the last time I lived in a closet to protect my family and myself. A few students came out to me in private, but not many. As the Queer community has become more known and has been shown in a more positive light in popular

3. The ever-expanding letter combinations started with the simple but very complicated word *gay*. Then expanded to "gay and lesbian" language, but that language has expanded to include multiple options and at times it is difficult to determine which configuration to use so as not to exclude those who have been omitted for way too long, especially our two-spirit, pansexual, asexual, and questioning siblings.

4. Mechelke, "Call to Queerness."

culture and as more and more members of the community live fully and joyfully into their authentic Queer selves, things have shifted significantly. Now I start each course, no matter the topic or area of learning, asking folx to name and identify themselves as they feel comfortable, encouraging them to share whatever pronouns they use in their own lives. Naming and using appropriate pronouns have become important ways of establishing a tone for my courses, by acknowledging identity as a part of the learning and growing process. I would not dare ask that at Hood because it wasn't safe, and I was not "out" to the seminary administration and most of my students. Now that part of our initial course sharing, which evolves over the semester as students feel safer and more at ease expressing their whole self, happens in almost all of our classes here at United Lutheran Seminary. My belief is that professors, teachers, pastors, Sunday school teachers, and parents all need to be attentive to this desire to name and claim all of who their students, children, and friends are as part of the Queer community. But many in that community still do not hear that fluidity in defining moments. Queer folx still do not hear "siblings" or "family of choice" from their family, let alone in their church. Instead, they hear "brothers and sisters," which is painful for those who identify beyond that binary language. They need to hear words and pronouns as affirmations in the church because it is vital both for those in the Queer community and for those who need their horizons broadened beyond limitations of heteronormality.

The alphabet soup comes as a part of that naming and claiming. Whereas LGBT was the only thing I knew, now the expansive language and understanding of identity leads to a drilling down to the deepest and broadest framing of identity. The four letters of my adult life—LGBT—have been retired. For the most part how many letters and the order of them continues to change, it seems. Those letters and the word *Queer* that I currently find appropriate for my personal, pastoral, and public usage, are important, but they also may change as the community continues to define itself. Lesbian, gay, bisexual, and transgender identities have been very well-known. Over the last decade the idea of limiting gender to only two definitions has proven to be a false position. As broader understandings of sexual orientation and gender binary and nonbinary identities have entered our cultural awareness, the truth is gender and gender expressions are more than any alphabet can describe. Gender is what a Queer or straight person understands as their gender, but so can a Two Spirit, Indigenous person who lives into a male, female, and intersex sexuality in their sense of self and the activities they participate in despite gender norms. Then there is the pansexual, someone who is attracted to persons regardless of their gender. Sexuality, one's understanding of who they are attracted to sexually, has evolved. One's gender expression is how a Queer person presents themselves in the world, through their hair, clothing, or other physical expressions. I am a lesbian and my birth gender is female. I understand my sexuality to mean I am attracted to women. I present more and more as I age in a nonbinary way. The expansive realities of this community have allowed me to break some of the learning that was taught formally and informally to me as I grew up about being in public appropriately. I was taught to wear a dress to church, not to have tomboy hair, and never to wear men's clothing. Some of that learning was spoken but it was also so normative that moving outside of those expectations was seen as abnormal, and I knew it from my sisters and the jokes made about my attire in high school by classmates. I also heard it from my dad, who was not happy when I wore old jeans, untied sneakers, and feminist T-shirts, and that I kept my hair shorter than my sisters.

Today I say BS to all of that. Every person should have the ability and opportunity to express their gender and gender expression without fear and proudly in public. *Should* is the operative word there. However, it isn't always safe to live our lives out loud. Queer folx brace themselves and arrive with caution in public spaces. There is a level of preparation needed in the world when we are fully our authentic selves—our Queer, Black, Latinx, Indigenous, gender nonconforming folx wearing what makes them comfortable, those who are a little or a lot heavy or thin and toned bodies glistening in the sun, drag queens or drag kings "werking it," gay bears with hairy chests proudly paraded down by the Fire Island beach, or the granola-crunching lesbians in their Prius on the boulevard near my home, with two dogs in the backseat. Being our true selves can be dangerous. And none of us are defined by one thing. We have "hyphenated/comma identities." White, Queer, nonbinary gender expression, highly educated, pastor, professor, solidly middle class, married with an internationally adopted child—that's me. But I don't drive a Prius or have dogs in my back seat. My identity comes with privilege that others in our community don't have. Queer kids complete suicides at a much higher rate their straight counterparts, and I want you to understand that Black trans women are killed in a significantly higher proportion than their white counterparts.[5] We are not safe. At the time of writing this book a lesbian shop owner was gunned down over a dispute about the Pride flag she refused to take down in front of her shop.[6] These are scary times, still.

However, there are places where we do feel a little bit safer. We do walk into safer spaces—gay clubs, resort locales, exclusively gay cruises, and friends' holiday parties—with a flair and a freedom that few other spaces provide. It really doesn't matter where we are outside of those rather safe locations; still, we brace, we prepare, and we step gingerly into spaces that for us, now or in the past, make us feel unsafe. However, as a white woman I do not have to face the fear that our Black, Latinx, and Indigenous folx face in so many places that are not safe. This feeling of being unsafe, unfortunately, also happens to Queer folks in the church. The fear is not only about what they will or will not hear from the pulpit, it also manifests in the looks that some "church people" throw at them in religious spaces. Church folx can and often do react negatively to the appearance and manner of dress, hair style, piercings, and/or visible tattoos on Queer bodies who venture into church. This is a huge deterrent to the community being even willing to walk into

5. Schoenbaum, "Report."

6. Laura Ann Carleton was fatally shot Friday outside Mag.Pi, the clothing and home decor shop she owned in Cedar Glen, a mountain community east of Los Angeles. See Associated Press, "California shop owner killed."

church spaces. It should feel safe but too often it is not. This is the reason I wrote this book. Transformation in a preacher's sermon or in the welcome received when entering a religious space can be the first sign of safety in the space.

A significant part of the pain inflicted by the church comes in the "bashing" felt not only in the language of the church but in the core values that far too often have not included those who are not heteronormative. And it comes in the continued use of "clobber passages"[7] from the Bible that parts of the church use as a tool for condemnation and to justify an unwillingness to speak to the Queer community using language that is positive and affirming.

The scope of this book seeks to mitigate some of the exclusive and condemning practices that are present in the church today and are still proclaimed from church pulpits. My intent is to encourage and provide a framework from which pastors and preachers can proclaim a gospel of grace and love. And I want to help Queer folx begin to heal from the wounds inflicted upon them by the church and by church people.

In chapter 1, I will begin with my story. I've lived this reality and I know firsthand the pain and fear associated with coming out and the stigma of rejection and exclusion present in the church for most of its history. Approaching these issues as a preaching professor makes sense. It is vital to proclaim a word from the pulpits of our faith communities that is live-giving, restorative, and speaks clearly against the language of hate and rejection. I tell my story, which is like the journey of so many of my Queer siblings, to bring a word of hope and offer new possibilities of G_d's love. Hopefully this self-disclosure will ignite in you a desire to tell your own story or by reading it you can better relate to members of the Queer community who may be part of your faith community or who might want to be married or have their child baptized or have entered into your space because they have encountered your

7. The typical list of Scripture which are often used to exclude and condemn Queer persons varies, but I will be centering on these addressing several of these texts in chapter 3–4. They are Genesis 19, Leviticus 18:22 and 20:13, and Romans 1: 26–27. My source for some of this work is Martin, *Unclobber*.

community at Pride events or by hosting a drag bingo night or by reading your core values on your church web page. What you say matters. What you proclaim can be liberating or condemning. So is your silence. Which will you choose? Which will you proclaim?

Next, I turn in chapter 2 to the historical and cultural reality of Queer existence. Ideas of exclusion and rejection did not happen in a vacuum, and they did not just turn up in the twentieth century. They were encountered in early history, in the writings and laws of those time periods, and through religious interpretations of appropriate gender appearance and behavior related to one's sexuality. The search of the past makes for a foundation that brings us to a deeper understanding around the issues of today's cultural and religious reactions to Queer lives. The old adage may be right: if we refuse to look at our past, we are doomed to repeat those mistakes again and again. I want you to be on the right side of history and to be a force for inclusion and grace. Someone is counting on you and your community of faith and you may never know who they are or how they found you or your church, but they are listening and wanting the love of a G_d who transforms judgment into hope and moves from exclusion to inclusion to be part of the word for the day.

Chapter 3 addresses one of the most pressing issues around this topic—the use of biblical texts to damage and abuse Queer folx. The use of "clobber passages" to beat up the Queer community has been happening for centuries. We can only move forward if we open our minds and hearts to the process of reviewing the traditional interpretation of biblical texts with a clearer sense of the context of the times and a deeper dive into the theology of love and grace when reading or using these texts alongside texts of grace, love, and acceptance taught by Jesus. Interpretation of these texts (often misinterpretations, I believe) along with unhelpful and incorrect contextualization of these texts have laid the foundation for a climate of hate and mistrust within faith communities toward the Queer community. Seeing these texts in a new light can bring about not only a new understanding of the reader's own view of Scripture but can also bring about intentional transformation in religious communities and give preachers skills to proclaim a new word based on the theology and understanding that comes from seeing these texts in a new light.

Creating or recreating a theology of inclusion and affirmation is the primary underpinning of this book and specifically occurs in chapter 4. The reader is invited to enter a new safer and braver place in their preaching, teaching, advocacy, and lives. The idea that we can actually create safe space for everyone is a fallacy. We instead need to create brave spaces where questions can be asked and where answers can be new learnings about ancient texts that have long been used as a battering ram toward not just the Queer community, but against others as well. Living out of the closet and living proudly as a Queer person or as a Queer advocate, or as a Queer companion on the journey, is sacred and vital work. Having a sense of what that looks like in our present age—when over five hundred anti-gay, anti-trans, and racist laws are being enacted across the country—means this work must happen *now*. And preachers and religious leaders must speak out and lift up the Queer community in every way they can. Understanding and articulating a theology of acceptance is a deeply personal journey but then it also is a communal transformation that needs to happen. I used to hope for tolerance. That's not enough. I don't want to be tolerated as a Queer person or for the church to simply tolerate the existence of Queer folx. What is needed is a reassessment of the theology that got the church to this point in the first place. And to chart a new theology with a pathway to inclusivity and affirmation.

Chapter 5 asks the preacher to exegete (study the text) for preaching in a new way. I want those speaking in churches and in public spaces as "public theologians" to craft sermons in ways that lift up and affirm Queer persons and challenge previous understandings of Queer lives. The book provides a new approach to preaching that shifts the thinking and the focus of our sermon preparation. What I offer is a "sexegetical" approach to crafting sermons that deal deeply, authentically, and intentionally with the historical, cultural, biblical, and theological hurdles negatively impacting Queer folx that have been in use for most of history. That is hard work, but work that must be done, I believe.

Chapter 6 will not only echo the themes in this book but will also provide the reader with a case study of a church connecting to a Queer community in the Deep South. The small church was brave enough to suggest hosting a "Drag Me To Church" event in collaboration with the Atlanta Pride Community. Their goal was to provide a safe and brave space to welcome, preach, sing, and hear a Word that proclaimed the grace of G_d to the amazing community that gathered in their small church in Georgia. Part of the opening of the service was to say "*I am sorry for the pain that the church has caused and we commit with you to keep working on transforming the church to truly embrace you—every bit of you.*" This is the Word of the *Lord*. So was ending the service singing together with a drag queen "We Are Family," by Sister Sledge. That's holy stuff.

This book will challenge you and make you reconsider parts of your understanding about the Queer community and the work that all of us need to do. We have the opportunity to craft a new reality of Queer acceptance—not simply to be marginally tolerated. I want to be affirmed for all of who I am. So do my Queer siblings, and I commit myself and my work to help bridge the divide that is still part of way too many faith communities. We can change—our minds, our hearts, and our embodiment of Christ's church. We can . . . and we must.

Chapter One

Telling My Story

I WAS BORN IN 1962 in West Texas to a preacher and a teacher. I have two sisters—one a year older and one a year younger. The three of us were often put into the Christmas plays as the "three Wisemen." They thought it was funny. It drove me up the wall. I wanted to be a shepherd so I could wear pants, wear a cool bath robe, wrap a towel around my head, and carry a big stick. Every year we were the three Wisemen, and every year I cried a little inside. The boys got to be shepherds because they were boys. That made me angry and began my development as a feminist in a very masculine-oriented, "cowboy tough" environment. I thought there had to be female shepherds out there. My sister, Karla, finally spoke up for herself at the age of seven and said she wanted to play Mary. Our Christmas pageant director was not amused. But we fought for what we wanted, and we prevailed through the advocacy of my sister. From that point forward Karla was Mary, I was a dusty-robed shepherd carrying a shepherd's staff, and Kim got to be an angel. That moment taught me about advocating for myself more openly. It was a great lesson.

The truth is I rebelled from the normative practice of being a typical girl—wearing a dress, playing with girl toys, wanting anything to do with the Barbie world, and wearing pink or lace—from a very young age. My maternal grandmother, Nanny, was a seamstress and during that time dresses were often made by mothers or grandmothers for their granddaughters if money was tight. Nanny loved to use the same pattern in three different colors and sizes, so that the three of us matched. Sometimes there were lace or bows on the dresses. I hated all of it. I told Nanny and my mom when I was about four that I was a "different kind of girl than my sisters." Lace, bows, and dresses were not what I wanted to be seen in. I spoke my truth and they listened. They agreed to no pink, no bows, and no lace. It took a bit longer to say no to all the dresses, but it finally happened.

My parents didn't fully understand at the time that I truly was a different kind of girl. I didn't either. They bought me a Tumbling Tomboy for my fifth birthday. The Tumbling Tomboy tumbled using an early edition of a wired controller and all I wanted in the world was that "doll" that had tomboy hair and clothes. They also bought me a cowboy outfit and one day I threw a huge fit to get to wear it to church. A few eyebrows were raised when I came down the center aisle of the sanctuary with my chaps, six-shooters in a holster, and cowboy hat on as my spurs jangled on the linoleum floor. That wouldn't be the last time I stirred the pot with my clothing choices. I had a T-shirt in high school that said, "A woman needs a man like a fish needs a bicycle." How did so many people not get the hint? My father was not amused by the shirt or by my refusal to wear anything but jeans, a T-shirt, and untied shoelaces on my tennis shoes. I was asserting a bit of control and it felt liberating even though it caused issues with my dad. The only person who knew I was gay at that time was rev. h sharon howell, my mentor and dear friend, who I confided in when I was sixteen years old. I only told her because the secret was tearing a hole in my soul. I needed to say the words "I'm gay" to another living being so badly that I was literally sick to my stomach every day of my teenage years. I threw up at school because I was so anxious about my secret. I played at being happy and I did excel in a number of areas as a kid and as I grew into high school to fit in a bit better.

sharon was a safe refuge for me as my "person" to share the secrets from my life. I had said the words to my Billie Jean King poster in my bedroom but that was as far as I had gone with that disclosure. I knew in my heart that part of my very being was considered inherently bad. I heard it in the small West Texas town where we were living during junior high and high school and on the news as people reacted to protests and the gay liberation movement that was gaining ground. All I knew was I better not tell anyone. I heard kids in the halls call each other "fags" or "dykes" or "homos." I heard it when I fell asleep on the band bus on the shoulder of my best friend Beth. I heard it in the language of my church, decided on by an international body of United Methodists. Those words were thrown in my direction many times and I laughed and said, "Not me." I didn't hear any positive reactions to being gay on any level in my life. I understood who I knew myself to be was considered wrong, unacceptable, and sinful. The language of my denomination said being gay was "incompatible with Christian teaching."[1] That's a powerful statement to wrap your head around.

One of the most painful moments for me was when my mother told me "The day you came out to me was the worst day of my life." She told me this during a really good time for us. She was honest and shared that feeling with me. She wanted to show me how far she had come, but it still hurt knowing that was how she felt for a number of years. I also had to acknowledge that she

1. *The Book of Discipline of the United Methodist Church, 2012.* Homosexuality first appeared in *The United Methodist Book of Discipline* in 1972. The current paragraph includes the following: "¶ 304.3 Qualifications for Ordination. While persons set apart by the Church for ordained ministry are subject to all the frailties of the human condition and the pressures of society, they are required to maintain the highest standards of holy living in the world. The practice of homosexuality is incompatible with Christian teaching. Therefore, self-avowed practicing homosexuals[1] are not to be certified as candidates, ordained as ministers, or appointed to serve in The United Methodist Church.[2]" This language was changed during the General Conference of the UMC in May, 2024, however I grew up with that exclusive language and practice for the vast majority of my life.

1. *"Self-avowed practicing homosexual"* is understood to mean that a person openly acknowledges to a bishop, district superintendent, district committee of ordained ministry, board of ordained ministry, or clergy session that the person is a practicing homosexual. See Judicial Council Decisions 702, 708, 722, 725, 764, 844, 984, 1020.

2. See Judicial Council Decisions 984, 985, 1027, 1028.

didn't know anything different. She did not grow up in a world where people were "out" to their families or friends. She was grieving what she anticipated for my life and how unsafe it might be for me to live my truth. She didn't have resources or people to process it with. She is so far from that moment today and we share a deep emotional connection that blesses me every day. I wonder what her experience would have been if she had those resources. I also wonder what my life might have been if I had access to the plethora of online and printed materials that are available today to Queer folx coming out or just beginning to understand themselves to be gay, lesbian, transgender, bisexual, gender nonconforming, or all the evolving understandings about issues related to Queer or questioning persons. Recently Susan,[2] a teenager in my church, came out to me. I was in tears for them and for their boldness to claim who they are and share it with another person at that age. She was taking her girlfriend to prom and she wanted me to know who she was finding herself to be. Later she asked if I could do her wedding when she got to that point in her life. I stood there crying and holding her in a big mama bear hug. It took me back to that hushed and fearful phone call to sharon to tell her I was gay. Before I made that call, I checked the door to make sure no one was near who might hear my conversation. I was terrified of the reaction I might get. This time, with Susan, I was on the other end of the telling. She was beaming with pride and joy in discovering who she is and in taking the risk, in high school, to ask a same-sex person on a date. Creeping into that conversation with her was my hope of a grand disclosing for her living fully and authentically into her life that I didn't have in my own. Susan wanted to be understood for her own holiness and to receive a blessed sense of affirmation, not just from family members, because some knew and others didn't yet, but from others in their life, like me. Every teenager feels shame, embarrassment, and confusion. It's part of growing up and finding who we are. Some unfortunately have adults in their lives telling them they are fundamentally defective if they are Queer. I told her the words I did not hear for so long in my own life. I tried

2. Not her name and shared anonymously, with her permission.

to echo my friend, sharon, when I spoke into her heart and soul. I told Susan that defective crap is not true. I spoke truth into that young person to provide a possibility of life and love. It was clear that we had created a safe and brave space for folx in our church and in my relationship with Susan that created the space for her to disclose that truth. I say the same thing to Queer folx every chance I get. Don't let anyone take away your joy or your understanding of who you are. You are a beloved child of G_d. You are amazing . . . just as you are. Psalm 139:14 (NRSV) states:

> I praise you, for I am fearfully and wonderfully made.
> Wonderful are your works; that I know very well.

I watched as Susan's face radiated even more broadly with a huge smile. What if I was told that message early on, that I was a wonderful work of G_d? What if? I can't go back in time to get a do-over, but I can remember my own life lessons and grow from there. I can also be that person for others. That is one of the surprising things in how my faith and pastoral vocation emerged.

Church was a huge part of growing up as a Wiseman. My dad was a pastor, all of my grandparents went to church, most of my aunts and uncles went to church, and my parents met at a Christian college through a former pastor of my mom's who had moved to the hometown of my dad. That pastor suggested they meet. The rest is history. Good times and bad times. Three girls to raise. Two careers to manage. And countless athletic and band activities to deal with. They had three daughters with very different personalities and different understandings of themselves. It couldn't have been easy.

My dad preached on Sundays at the numerous United Methodist churches where he served throughout his sixty-plus years of ministry. He did not preach any hate toward gay people, but I heard the language of he or she, sisters and brothers exclusively. My dad was preaching in the 1970s and 1980s as I was coming to understand myself as a lesbian. I knew no other soul in my high school or in my church travels as a youth representative for our denomination who were gay and open in the church. When anti-gay language was voted into the *Discipline* of the UMC in 1972, I was barely aware as I was only ten years old. It did not make a splash in the media, nor did it affect how my friends and church folx talked about the grace of G_d. I became aware only when I was told at a regional gathering of youth several years later that any "self-avowed and practicing homosexual"[3] would be excluded from pastoral ministry. I had to figure out what that meant. Basically, it meant "don't tell anyone." It meant, I guessed at the time, that if you were good enough at being a lesbian that you did not need to "practice" anymore (it's still a joke I make every so often with UMC friends). I figured out what the words meant, and it hurt deeply into the marrow of my bones. The evolution and journey to acceptance of my sexuality, albeit a secret one, began to influence how I viewed my role in the world and potentially in the church. My exclusion from pastoral ministry—which I was just beginning to experience as a calling on my life—was being legislated by a huge international gathering that impacted the UMC substantially and was impacting me as well. Why was G_d calling me into a role in the church that my denomination was forbidding me to participate in? Why was being me so disgusting to others? Did G_d make me who I am or did some cosmic mistake happen to first make me gay and then place me in a catch-22 situation in the role I believed G_d was calling me to answer? It was frustrating and began to really impact my willingness to do anything with my faith. I went off to college determined to chart my own course. I went into my academic advisor's office at McMurry College, where both of my parents and both of my sisters went for a time during college, for my first advising session of my freshman year. My advisor (someone who knew me and my family well) had a "pre-seminary" course schedule already created for me to simply sign. I was angry and frustrated. So many people were making assumptions about who I was and who I was to become, and I felt like I had no choice in the matter, and none of them knew who I really was and how much shame I felt about myself. They had no idea I was harboring

3. *The Book of Discipline of the United Methodist Church, 2012,* ¶ 304.3 Qualifications for Ordination.

a secret that I was a "bad seed" and that if that secret was disclosed it would shatter my family and my life. I still thought that I did not deserve G_d's grace. I left McMurry and ended up in the education department of Texas Tech University, majoring in history and political science with a certificate in secondary education. When I graduated from college, I started teaching high school students world and American history and civics/government. I felt like I was right where I was supposed to be—loving teaching and my students. Maybe this was a new calling on my life. Maybe this was how I was to impact others—especially youth—through grace and care as a teacher during the time of my students' lives that was especially painful in my own high school experience. Maybe this was what was intended all along. But maybe I was taking a detour from where I was intended to be and maybe G_d might continue to nudge me more and more forcefully into the ministry. I wasn't sure because I was very confused. Of course, I never let my students know who I was, nor did I share that secret with my teaching friends. There was still something undesirable and "less than" in my mind about who I was.

I was teaching in the mid-eighties and the AIDS crisis was full-blown. I secretly went to a gay bar in town during that time. It was shady in every way possible. They had a back entrance and closely monitored the required verbal codes for admittance. I met a few gay men who I became friends with. One was Brian. He had no family who welcomed him home at holiday gatherings and was on his own in the world. Probably the feelings of being lost created the electricity of our friendship. We saw movies together and enjoyed each other's company. One day he called and told me he had tested positive for AIDS, called "gay cancer" by some. It was a death sentence at that time. I encouraged him to seek out his family to try to reconnect. He tried. They refused to even speak to him. So, I became part of his care team. I remember the progression of the disease and how he was simply melting away in front of me. As he got nearer to the end, he was hospitalized with AIDS-related pneumonia and several other complicating issues that I knew were terminal. I remember a visit a few weeks prior to his death. He was skin and bones. I was required to put on a hospital gown, gloves, and a face mask to visit him on the AIDS wing of the hospital (this was protective gear that came back as required behavior during the COVID pandemic, and it took me back to that time with my friend). I sat on the bed next to him and talked. I talked about movies and told stories. As I was preparing to leave, he asked with tears running down his cheeks if I would hold his hand. I had been doing that for most of the visit, so I thought he wanted me to hold his hand one last time. He looked up at me and said, "I have not touched or been touched by a human hand for weeks. Please hold my hand." I took my gloves off and held his hands and touched his face. Both of us were crying and in my heart, I knew I was potentially endangering myself, but I didn't care. When he died, no one called to let me know that he died.

That need for human connection was deeply missing in my life, too. Mine was not physical contact, mine was a craving to be more fully known for all of who I was. Many Queer folx have very problematic relationships with their families. I wanted to be known fully by my family and friends. During my next visit home, I came out to my parents. It did not go well. I said it with anger and did not give them any time to process before they were ready to respond. Yelling, "I'm gay, deal with it," and storming out of the house was not my best moment. I would come out to them two additional times over the next few years before they heard me and before I heard them. It has taken time to finally gain more and more understanding and acceptance.

I had been processing this fact since I was a small girl asking for a cowboy—not cowgirl—outfit, through those painful and hate-filled years of junior high and high school, and through my early twenties trying to make a place in the world where I never really felt seen or heard. I was giving my parents a few moments to respond. It wasn't fair. But it was a beginning. That first leap off the high dive into unknown waters is a journey Queer folx too often take on their own. There is no usual response, there is no typical timeline or a perfect way to present one's sexuality or gender identity to their friends and family. It is always scary and anxiety-producing. It is never complete in one conversation. It can take years to begin to resolve and for too many, like Brian, there is not enough time to wait, and for some resolution never happens. Queer folx hope and dream, just like their straight siblings, of a happy ending that too often isn't possible. Some have no family to be there for that dive. Some are accepting of their Queer family members or friends readily. That process has become somewhat easier for some in the community over the past few decades, but many others still find hatred and rejection as the only response. They hear the old religious and biblical prejudices that say, "You're a mistake. You're fundamentally bad. You're not good enough. You're a sinful mess." Been there, heard that, and didn't buy the T-shirt. However, it's imprinted deeply on my body, in my mind, and is part of my soul—still.

The same desire for a moment of acceptance, affirmation, and grace happens for many folx in their dealings with the church. Maybe they grew up in the church and they were never fully able to be themselves. Maybe they tried and the door was slammed in their face because of their gender, sexuality, or expression of who they are. Still others have no relationship with the church and have no illusions that a positive relationship with the church might happen for them. Decade upon decade the church has sent the message that members of the Queer community were not welcome and that their presence was barely tolerated if they played the organ or if they could direct or sing in the choir.

I had a conversation with my dad about this when he was serving as associate pastor for visitation in Lubbock, Texas at the First United Methodist Church. It is a large, tall-steeple, down-town church in West Texas where the Dallas Cowboys, country music, and church were and still are huge. It was a trinity of sorts and being different meant I was not ever going to be part of that trinity. I was visiting there one Sunday, a number of years after my traumatic coming-outs had leveled off. The soloist that day was a young man who immediately sent my "gaydar"[4] pinging,

4. Many in the Queer community believe they can "sense" another Queer person when they meet and sometimes just by seeing each other across a

whose presence called to who I was in that moment. I thought, he's "family" as a Queer person. Now this was an assumption, but it proved to be true when I checked with my dad after the service. I then asked if his church was moving toward being an open and affirming church in the UMC since they had clearly opened their choir to Queer folx. The designation would send a clear statement of welcome to the LGBTQIA+ community. His reply about this was simply, "No, but we welcome him and others to sing in our choir or come to church." I pushed further, "Dad if he has a partner and they have/adopt a baby and want that child baptized during the 10 am televised service, would that be okay?" I knew from the delay in his response that I had my answer. He further explained it would have to be approved by the senior pastor, the pastoral staff, and the church council and possibly even cleared with the bishop. It was the Northwest Texas Annual Conference of The United Methodist Church—part of the belt buckle of the Bible Belt. My reply was, "Then you're not fully welcoming." They never would have gone through so many processes for a straight couple wanting their child baptized during that service. I think it was eye-opening for both of us.

That's the response that many in the Queer community have experienced in the church. There is not a full answer to their question—"Will you love and let me be *me* in your church?" The emphatic "no" is sometimes easier to understand than the qualified "No—," described in the book, *Dear God, I Am Gay—Thank You!* In it I found a wonderful image of the flipped relationship many in the Queer community experience in the church.[5] The Gospel of Luke is my favorite gospel due to its multiple stories of women and Jesus caring for the people on the edge of society. In Luke's Gospel there is a profound inclusive love that he proclaims from

---

room. I have just nodded to someone I thought was gay and they do the same back to me with a smile on their face. We often "know" each other in that moment. Some call it instinct and others call it a gift honed over years of hiding who we are and we learn to see another in pain and acknowledge it. Obviously, it can also be way off, especially when the other person is not yet out or when you are just plain wrong.

5. Workin, *Dear God, I Am Gay*, 4–5.

the life and lessons of Jesus. A favorite story of mine from Luke is the story of the prodigal son, only told in that gospel. There are several characters that one can identify with: the waiting parent, the jealous and angry older sibling, and the impatient and petulant younger sibling. Often this text is preached in a way that says G_d is the patient, waiting, and welcoming parent—loving us for all of who we are and welcoming anyone who has strayed back into the home and the arms of that patient and loving parent. Sermons assuming their listeners and/or their church were either the older or younger sibling are common. Some choose to ignore who they might be and focus instead on G_d's amazing patience with us, no matter what character we are playing in the world. These sermons often sound hollow, or they were used as battering rams to bludgeon those they felt and were told they were a "petulant and sinful child" or "an angry and jealous child" with the preacher, on behalf of the church, making the decision of who was playing these roles in the story. These sermons use the brokenness of the Queer community against them. These sermons, first, directly or indirectly, cast Queer lives and bodies as petulant and sinful, running off to squander all that the loving parent had provided them. They utilize the story to advocate to bring Queer folx back into the arms of the loving and patient parent. All "we" needed to do was acknowledge the innate sinfulness of our lives and to turn our backs on the "sinful living" we were engaged in. All we needed to do was change our "preference." I call bullshit. This is not a healthy or helpful reading of the story. And it endangers Queer folx by perpetuating this lie.

According to Joel R. Workin, in his book *Dear God, I Am Gay—Thank You!*, the Queer community instead assumes the role of patient parent to a church that has "taken the journey to the far country" and left Queer folx behind.[6] The church is "off living its carnal and sinful life" of rejecting the human and wonderfully made reality of Queer lives. The church left the Queer community who were/are part of a faith community or spiritual expression, waiting and waiting, never sure if the church will ever return and restore the relationship. Workin uses Kierkegaard in framing this

6. Workin, *Dear God, I Am Gay*, 4.

thought. Kierkegaard asks his readers to "imagine a compound word which lacks the last word: there is only the first word and the hyphen."[7] For the Queer community, the reversal of the story and the reality of waiting on a church that said, "No, period" has left us beaten, bloodied, and burdened by the guilt and shame often inflicted on the Queer community by both the institutional church and Christians whose beliefs and judgment lead to some serious oppression, abuse, and hatred.

In my experience, the church, my church, The United Methodist Church, said an emphatic "NO, period" in 1972 and continues to reaffirm that NO, repeatedly when its international governing body has met every four years.[8] The No is loud and clear. I've heard it repeatedly. This "NO, period" was not just spoken in the church, but also in the world. The "NO, period" is a blunt and unwelcoming end of the hope for a Queer affirming church. The unfinished "No—" with the missing last word allows hope and possibility, according to Workin and Kierkegaard. I've just never felt the full possibility of the incomplete compound word in my church. It has been a "NO, period." It often feels like the church won't even consider the unfinished thought without fighting or again staking claim to an old understanding of the Bible, human history, or theology of exclusion. It gets old.

The waiting and hoping for the church to get its "shit" together finally wore me out. I couldn't live in the "NO, period" anymore. In November of 2014, on a trip to San Diego, I asked my partner of twenty-two[9] years to marry me. This was before the *Obergefell* Supreme Court decision making gay marriage legal everywhere in the US in June of 2015,[10] but we were hopeful and did not publicly announce our engagement until August of 2015, the year we were married. Within two hours of posting the announcement on our

7. Workin, *Dear God, I Am Gay*, 5.

8. At the time of this writing, the UMC had not yet changed their stance.

9. We had been together for twenty-two years at the time that I proposed. We have now been together for thirty years, married for eight years.

10. *Obergefell v. Hodges*, decided and announced by the United States Supreme Court on June 26, 2015.

Facebook pages, my district superintendent, the regional pastoral supervisor for the UMC, let me know that I had "self-avowed that I was a practicing homosexual" in direct defiance of the *Book of Discipline* of the church. Regretfully but resolutely I had already begun the clergy transfer process to move to the United Church of Christ, but that message from my district superintendent meant my relationship with the church of my birth, the church where I was baptized and confirmed, the church my dad was a pastor in, and the church that had embraced my calling and ordained me to pastoral ministry of Word and Sacrament, was throwing me out. It was leaving me beside the road alone—but sadly also left many other Queer pastors, believers, and skeptics. It was over. Just like that. I knew it was coming. I had already begun to prepare to transition to another denomination. I had planned our wedding to not include my own father as his district superintendent told him if he helped in any way that they would charge him with defying the *Book of Discipline*. I still was not ready. I was not prepared for the pain and anguish I would experience sending the letter resigning from clergy membership in the Kansas East Annual Conference of the United Methodist Church, which I had been in a tug-of-war with for all my life. I could have fought back and made the denomination level official charges against me and take me to trial to kick me out. I did not want to spend the next year of my life—while preparing for the wedding of a lifetime—burdened by a church trial. I wanted my life to be filled with love and with wedding plans, guest lists, appetizer tastings, and deciding on a cake flavor and design. I also did not want that year of fighting to embroil my dad in a battle with his own church and faith. I chose the best route for me, my wife, and my family. I would make the same decision again. The UMC had booted me off the bus and left me on the side of the road for good. They were not coming back to me as I at times patiently waited for them to return from their sinful journey away from me. There is no going back for me or for them as this book is being written.[11]

11. As I write this in 2023, there is a split occurring in the United Methodist Church. A conservative branch called the Wesleyan Covenant Association

The great gift of G_d's love is grace. G_d loves and delights in all creatures great and small in our world. The great gift of G_d's love is an emphatic YES to all. When the church says, "No, period," when the church says, "No—," when the church says no in any way, G_d says YES! That is the grace of G_d that the Queer community, some of whom have by the skin of their teeth held on to some relationship with the divine or the church, needs to hear. For far too many, their connections to the church and to G_d have been severed, some by others' actions or the church's abusive behavior and some by their own act of reclaiming their call, personhood, and identity outside of the church. The use of sermons and lessons to wound others and especially to judge and inflict pain on the Queer community, intentionally or unintentionally, has left battle wounds too numerous to count.

The next part of this book will explore where the "No, period" to Queer people comes from and the possibilities of preaching a Gospel of love and acceptance that can bring healing to the brokenness of those left behind and those still in the pews hoping to hear a word of G_d's grace for them. It may even speak a word to those who have left or been run out of their church bodies. We live in hope.

---

is in the process of forming. About three hundred churches have voted to move out of the United Methodist Church to associate with the WCA. This conservative denomination is not and likely will not ever be inclusive of the LGBTQI2S+ community. Those who remain in the UMC are a diverse body of churches, pastors, members, and denominational leaders who will endeavor to remove the restrictive language about allowing Queer pastors to serve openly and about allowing same-sex marriages to take place in UMC churches and to be officiated by UMC pastors. At the present time, I have no intention to go back to this denomination. The scars run deep.

Chapter Two

A Brief History of Queer Lives in Context

I BEGIN THIS CHAPTER with a single underlying question with a variety of nuances and I offer some possible answers to the "No, period" reality that many in the Queer community experience in religious institutions. *What defines the historical relationship between Queer folx and the church? Is it hate? Is it avoidance? Is it rejection? Is it based on a "don't ask/don't tell" arrangement? Is it the complicated and often conflictual nature of the culture and religious relationship? Is it based on the "clobber passages" that are used from Scripture to vilify the Queer community? Or is it some combination of the above?* So many possibilities form the crux of that complicated relationship. And this journey may lead us to more questions than answers. But maybe, just maybe, we will find some answers together.

As you read in the first chapter, my own story with the church is complicated and is one of initial acceptance while keeping the secret; to discomfort about possibly being accidently "outed" by my son or other close friends who knew the state of my relationship with my longtime partner, Cindy; to outright rejection from denominational leaders when our marriage was announced publicly; to my own decision to leave my church, the church of my birth, baptism, and the church where several generations of my family, including my father, were pastors. It was a process filled with great joy when I was ordained in 1995, to a more reserved role as more and more friends and family knew about our relationship beyond Cindy being a "good friend" who lived with me to care for my son (yes, people did think that), to a painful end in 2015 that left me wounded and threatened to tear me from the church forever. I waited for the petulant child/squanderer of their inheritance, who went away. They just weren't going to come back.

My journey is one that has a lot of twists and turns, and that story is like many other Queer folx in and out of the church. In the vastness of Christian history and even in the times of the Hebrew people, as described in the Torah, homosexuality[1] has always been complicated, to say the least. Jesus never spoke about what we would understand as homosexuality in the twenty-first century, as attitudes have shifted over the centuries and have rapidly changed during the past few decades. Understanding the complex history of homosexuality is beyond the scope of this book; however, we can explore some notable shifts and misunderstandings.

Jewish people, like their later siblings in the faith, Christians, have been molded by their history, a history that contains laws regulating sexual behavior and traditions that directed the social and cultural expectations of their followers. Any book that includes a people's historically complex relationships, especially around the issue of homosexuality, must start at the beginning. I have, more times than I can count, seen people on picket lines and on their social media feeds saying, "God made Adam and Eve. Not Adam and Steve." Westboro Baptist Church, a church in Topeka, Kansas, which protests anything related to Queer issues came to protest me at my church in 1996, Grandview United Methodist in Kansas City, Kansas, because I dared to speak for gay rights within the UMC in the religion section of the *Kansas City Star*. I saw those same signs and other more hateful and graphic signs that

---

1. While this phrase elicits strong responses from some, for the purposes of this book I use it to describe the general understating of same-gender sexual behavior. Other phrases that are used include same-gender loving persons or same-sex partnered relationships.

accompanied their presence outside my church during our worship service. Every time I hear those words, Adam, Steve, or Eve, they trigger something inside of me. From my experience within the Queer community those words do the same thing to others.

While it is a biblical fact that the story told in the first two chapters of Genesis indicates that G_d did indeed create Adam and Eve, it was certainly not the end of the story. Placing these signs or posting these words serves as another reminder that Queer folx are considered deviant creations far from G_d's intention or grace. The use of the word "God" on their signs and posts indicates that anyone—Adam and Steve or Pam and Eve—are not part of G_d's plan. The language in the modern context excludes trans, nonbinary, and genderqueer members of the Queer community.[2] It is complicated by the gender roles assumed in ancient cultures, like Israel. Language for gender in the Torah provided male and female as the only options. The possibility for other expressions of gender fluidity was not present. The primary roles of males and females often limited males to providing the primary security of the property and home, while women typically managed the home and were responsible for procreation.[3] Obviously these roles overlapped and likely were not the absolute reality of ancient peoples. There were outliers in the ancient world and outliers are present in the modern world, as well. Evidence from our own modern and complex relationships with one another shows how assumed gender roles are switched or shared in significant ways. That same language and those same assumptions about gender and sexuality greet Queer siblings time after time in the modern world and in different but similar provocative meanings in different words used to describe them. I have been asked more times than I can count by friends and a few family members, "How do you decide who gets to be the 'man' in your relationship every day?" Jokingly I respond, "We tossed a coin this morning and she won. She gets to be the girl today." Being in a same-gender, loving, long-term relationship doesn't make sense to these questioners. They see

2. Finke, *Queerfully and Wonderfully Made*, 16.

3. Durgen and Johnson, eds., *Biblical World of Gender*, xvii–xviii.

being lesbians or anyone else on the Queer spectrum as a "choice" that we could change if we really tried hard enough. For them our relationships are considered "abnormal," since they fall outside of their experience or understandings. These nosy and uninformed friends and family members want to see a male and female expression of partnership using the "traditional heteronormative expectations" for those gender assumptions. For our trans and gender-fluid siblings this kind of inquiry literally dismisses their very existence. Assumptions can be frustrating. Assigned gender roles can be shortsighted and limiting. Language equating the Queer community as being divergent from the divine's plan leaves lasting wounds and gets played out in culture and unfortunately in the church frequently.

As complex as things are today, homosexuality was also complicated for the Hebrew people. Some Hebrews accepted homosexuality outright. The word did not exist and the understanding of that has no relationship to the same-sex loving sexuality we know of today. Mixed messages in both the holy texts and the reality of what we might call "Queer" communities existed then and those mixed messages continue today. The question I am asking is, where do the laws denouncing same-gender relationships come from? A look at Hebrew texts can guide Christians and others on this quest. We start with the assumption that is often spouted but not accurate in what these texts perceive to be okay and not okay for what we might call Queer Hebrew behavior. One assumption is that all same-gender behavior was unilaterally forbidden in the Hebrew Torah. However,

> Deuteronomy does not ban homosexuality, only sacred prostitution. So the question is, when was sex among men banned? We cannot know with accuracy. The ban only appears in two verses, both in the same section of Leviticus (18:22 and 20:13). Most scholars believe these verses were written either during the Babylonian Exile or during the early Second Temple period, so sometime during the 6th to the 4th century BCE (2600 to 2400 years ago), but when exactly in this period, we do not know. Nor can we know what led to this prohibition.

Some speculate that it was an expansion of the ban on sacred prostitution. Others think it was an effort to limit contact between Jews and gentiles, but the fact is no-one knows.[4]

In the next chapter I will be looking more closely at the texts that have been utilized to threaten and abuse the Queer community throughout time. As an example, the text of Leviticus 18:22 proves to be deeply problematic. In it a law is laid down regarding behavior between two males, "Do not lie with a male as one lies with a woman; it is an abhorrence." Reading that text in our modern context has led some to label homosexual behavior as something literally horrible and unacceptable. However, a deeper dive into the text reveals

> Biblical and ancient Near Eastern culture was not familiar in the sense of a defined sexual orientation or lifestyle [sic].[5] It acknowledges only the occasional act of male anal intercourse, usually as an act of force associated with humiliation, revenge, or subjection. And only a few Hebrew interpretations label it as an abominable act and a capital offense. It seems that Hebrew people view all sexual acts not potentially procreative as aberrant.[6]

However, the use of both male and female temple prostitutes was normative in the First Temple period. During the reign of King Rehoboam, the grandson of King David, "temple 'sodomites,'" as the King James Bible has it, were male and female sacred prostitutes: men and women who reside[d] in temples and had sex with patrons as a form of deity worship."[7] This practice was also found

---

4. Gilad, "Judaism and Homosexuality."

5. The use of the phrase "lifestyle" as part of the lexicon of Queer experience and assumptions again relies on the "preference" of the Queer person choosing a lifestyle. This language is inconsistent with both cultural and biological understandings. I only use this here with the notation.

6. Berlin and Brettler, *Jewish Study Bible*, 251–52. I will share more on the other "clobber passages" in the next chapter.

7. Gilad, "Judaism and Homosexuality."

in Canaanite, Mesopotamia, and Near Eastern cultures.[8] The practice was defined in a number of these cultures as another way to create "family" or to fulfill rites and observances for the people involved. There is evidence of the change to the status of persons engaging in same-sex relationships and sexual activities.

> From the end of the 4th century BCE, and later under the Romans, Jews found themselves living in cultures that practiced homosexuality between men and boys as a norm. The question is how tolerant the rabbis were of these practices. This turns out to be a very difficult question to answer. The all-important book of Jewish Law, the Talmud, contains statements to the effect that anal sex among men causes solar eclipses (Sukkah 29a) and earthquakes (Jerusalem Talmud, Berachot 13:3), but also distinguishes between two forms of pederasty—anal sex that warrants a penalty of death by stoning, and homosexual sex that doesn't involve penetration, about which the rabbis were more lenient (Niddah 13b). Oddly, to say the least, Jewish Law does not explicitly ban sex with boys under the age of nine (Talmud, Yevamot 51b, and Maimonides' Mishneh Torah, Biah 1:14, where he adds that in his opinion, the men should be flogged).[9]

While I refuse to believe that anal sex caused these traumatic "natural" events then, I do regretfully acknowledge that these beliefs around sexuality have often led to modern-day variations on this theme. Hurricanes in Florida have been blamed on Walt Disney World holding a "Gay Day" at their resort.[10] I also heard that Hurricane Sandy hit the East Coast in 2012 after president Barak Obama endorsed gay marriage. I've heard that Houston elected a lesbian mayor, so they were punished by Hurricane Harvey in 2017. These are more recent proclamations from conservative religious leaders and politicians. They are retelling the same lie from centuries before their time. Wherever they got the idea for these hateful accusations, sadly they continue to this day.

8. Gilad, "Judaism and Homosexuality."

9. Gilad, Judaism and Homosexuality.

10. Faughndur, "Inside the right's 'moral war against Disney.'"

Despite historic evidence, "many people consider homosexuality to be a modern-day phenomenon. This could not be further from the truth. Homosexuality has been documented in Western society as far back as the Ancient Greeks. Virtually every civilization since has had some record of the presence of homosexuality, from Ancient Greece to Rome to Victorian England, right up to the present day."[11] That history includes periods of hatred for the Queer community but seeing the roots of that hate is vital to this work. John Boswell states that despite a few who spoke negatively of homosexuality, with Plato being the primary negative voice, most in the ancient world did not condemn those with more flexible understandings of same-sex practice or love. This was possible because the understanding of an older man nurturing a younger man or boy sexually in Roman culture was seen as mentorship and not a sexual "relationship" or abusive behavior. Of interest to me is Boswell's statement that most of Western culture has come from Roman understandings on many issues around law, politics, culture, etc. However, this expansive understating of sexuality decidedly did not.[12] We are then left with the question of how the historical journey to the way we view things now has emerged. The Greeks of the classical period would have understood, "homosexuality and heterosexuality . . . as groups of not necessarily very closely related acts, each of which could be performed by any person, depending upon his or her gender [*sic*], status, or class."[13] They would not have defined someone solely based on who that person preferred to have a same-gender relationship with, as that would be unknown to them.

In Rome, homosexual relationships were common and even gay "marriage" was allowed. Some emperors had both female and male marriages. "There is absolutely no conscious effort on

---

11. Zive, "Brief History of Western Homosexuality."

12. Boswell, "Church and the Homosexual."

13. Duberman, Vicinus, and Chauncey Jr., *Hidden from History: Reclaiming the Gay and Lesbian Past*, 59. Even the title of this work uses binary language for gender. We have come a long way, especially recently, in understanding both gender and sexuality as more fluid realities than previously thought.

anyone's part in the Roman world, the world in which Christianity was born, to claim that homosexuality was abnormal or undesirable. There is in fact no word for 'homosexual' in Latin. 'Homosexual' sounds like Latin but was coined by a German psychologist in the late 19th century."[14] There were boundaries, however, in the ancient world.

> In some ways, Roman tolerance for homosexuality paralleled earlier Greek attitudes: so long as it was practiced in an 'appropriate' manner, homosexuality was acceptable. In Rome, this meant pursuing a young slave. By law, free youths were set off-limits. The Romans—like the Greeks —deplored freemen taking the 'passive' role in sexuality, as stated by the philosopher Seneca: "To be *impudicus* (that is passive) is disgraceful for a free man." For slaves, however, "There is nothing shameful in doing whatever the master orders." It was considered disgusting to continue sexual relations with a slave who was old enough to have facial hair, but not illegal.[15]

These boundaries were more social than legal, but that also meant there were extremely limited protections for Queer persons during that period. Younger or vulnerable males and females could be exploited easily, as well.

> The introduction of Christianity into the Roman world brought old Hebrew prejudices against homosexuality into the Empire. At first, it was tolerated—in fact, it was practiced by more than a few Roman Emperors. In the fourth century AD, a writer defended Constantine's continuation of the tax on homosexual prostitutes, saying that it allowed them to continue their practices with impunity. This tolerance, however, did not last. In 533 AD, homosexuality [*sic*] became entirely illegal in Rome. Emperor Justinian was known to castrate those found guilty of homosexuality [*sic*]. The laws on the books actually

---

14. Duberman, Vicinus, and Chauncey Jr., *Hidden from History*, 59. The use of the term *homosexual* in this chapter because it is language specific suitable to the task at hand.

15. Zive, "Brief History of Western Homosexuality."

proscribed death, but that punishment was generally not meted out.[16]

History continued to limit the role and acceptance of homosexual behavior. When the Roman Empire fell, homosexuality was plunged into the dark streets and private homes of those who were homosexual and those who sought out their services. Even though it was not illegal, the tolerance for gay persons was lost. In sixth-century Spain, we see the first real laws prohibiting homosexuality. They also prohibited Judaism and there are certainly links between the two sets of laws.[17] During the early part of the medieval period, homosexuality was tolerated and seldom prosecuted. "It was the writings of Thomas Aquinas that changed everything. In his writings, Aquinas described homosexuality as the worst of sexual sins. He argued that homosexual sex acts are the 'greatest sin among the species of lust' because they are contrary to the natural order of things as ordained by God."[18] The fact that the words of one man can change the acceptance, even though it might have been unspoken, of these persons so easily is one of the reasons for this book. Multiplying the understandings of current possibilities of acceptance, affirmation, and advocacy for Queer persons in the world, in the church, and from the pulpit is seriously needed. Turning to more modern Queer history in culture and faith, we turn, unsurprisingly, to the rise of Adolf Hitler and Nazism.

When I was in high school in Andrews, Texas, I read and heard the story of the Holocaust, which took the lives of over six million Jews. We learned about the rise of Adolf Hitler and Nazism. We heard the stories of our Jewish siblings' experience in Nazi Germany, and I wept. I was powerfully moved by the harrowing stories of Jews in and around Germany attempting to flee the country and sending their children to safety. The systematic persecution, arrest, and forced movement into Jewish ghettos, after stripping families of their homes and businesses, was inhumane.

16. Zive, "Brief History of Western Homosexuality."
17. Zive, "Brief History of Western Homosexuality."
18. Zive, "Brief History of Western Homosexuality."

The financial, political, and military persecution they endured is quite shocking to hear. The stories of soldiers rounding up Jews for transport on trains to concentration camps broke my heart. The forced separation of family members and collection of their belongings when they arrived in the camps was hard to bear.

However, there was one part of the story that I didn't read about in my history book, and it wasn't talked about in my high school history class—it was the discrimination, rounding up, torture, experimentation, and gassing of many homosexuals in those same concentration camps.

> Between 5,000 and 15,000 men were imprisoned in concentration camps as "homosexual" offenders. This group of prisoners was typically required to wear a pink triangle on their camp uniforms as part of the prisoner classification system. Many, but not all, of these pink triangle prisoners identified as gay.
>
> The pink triangle called attention to this prisoner population as a distinct group within the concentration camp system. According to many survivor accounts, pink triangle prisoners were among the most abused groups in the camps. Sometimes pink triangle prisoners were assigned the most grueling and demanding jobs in the camp labor system. They were often subjected to physical and sexual abuse by camp guards and fellow inmates. In some cases, they were beaten and publicly humiliated. In Buchenwald concentration camp, some pink triangle prisoners were subject to inhumane medical experiments. Beginning in November 1942, concentration camp commandants officially had the power to order the forced castration of pink triangle prisoners.[19]

Sixty percent of gay men sent to concentration camps were executed, a number that is actually higher than other groups executed in Nazi concentration camps. Why didn't I hear about this? Was West Texas just not ready to embrace those stories? I'm not sure. What I do know is when I entered my world history course my freshman year in college the issue was addressed, and I was

19. "Gay Men Under the Nazi Regime."

able to do a research paper on the round-up and criminalization of persons who were gay men and women or those suspected of that behavior, and the execution of so many Queer folx. Suddenly, I was hearing a new story. A story that impacted me more than I could imagine. One Holocaust survivor describes what he saw.

> "We saw barracks surrounded by a double circle of high fences . . . A torrent of blows awaited us. We were instantly overcome with terror." With these words in his 1994 memoir, Pierre Seel—one of the few gay Holocaust survivors to publicly share his experience—described his arrival at the Schirmeck-Vorbrück concentration camp on May 13, 1941. Having been arrested on account of his homosexuality in Nazi-occupied France, Seel was interrogated, tortured and forced to watch his lover being mauled by a pack of dogs—all before he'd even turned 18.[20]

The Nazis' understanding that the master race excluded Jews, deviants, gypsies, and homosexuals was absolute. It was a "No, period." There was zero tolerance. "Male homosexual behavior remained a crime even in East and West Germany, as well as in Great Britain, the United States, and the Soviet Union. Thus, the homosexual inmates in Nazi concentration camps were not considered to have been unjustly imprisoned, and therefore they remained uncompensated for their suffering."[21] During the next twenty years in Germany—East and West—male homosexuals could be reimprisoned. The ability of those in power both in the pre- and post-World War II world to deem persons of an entire race, gender, and/or sexuality to the status of being inhuman and unworthy of the very air they breathed is sadly still encountered just as it was almost eighty years ago. This is mind-blowing. The story has barely been told and so many suffered under this systematic prejudice and hatred of those different from the Nazi regime.

---

20. Carlo, "Why It Took Decades for LGBTQ Stories to Be Included in Holocaust History."

21. Duberman, Vicinus, and Chauncey Jr., *Hidden from History,* 373.

Again, part of the history of Queer lives and the church is the sheer volume of untold stories of faith and the inhumane treatment of their bodies, minds, souls, and relationships. Virtually all Queer people in the USA and many in the straight community know the story of the Stonewall riots, which began with a raid of the Stonewall Inn gay bar on June 28, 1969, in New York City. The gay bar was in Greenwich Village, an eclectic and diverse area of the city. The raid began, as others before it and others since, with the police entering the building and harassing those who frequented the bar: "transgender people, homeless youth, drag queens, gay men, and lesbians."[22] Unlike other responses to police raids around the country, that night the patrons of the bar fought back. They refused to be handcuffed. They would not be herded into the paddy wagons brought there for the police to round up as many people as possible for arrest and humiliation. The bar patrons threw bricks and pushed past the police line into the street. It was then that a kind of magic happened. Queer folx who lived closeted in their homes and apartments nearby heard the sirens and the cries of their Queer siblings, and came out to help. More and more joined the public protests each night after the raid. These protests went on for four nights. That historical event and what happened in the streets in New York and around the country formed the basis for the gay rights movement. The story of the Stonewall riots spread like wildfire across the country. Queer newspapers, word of mouth, and some national news coverage told the story of those refusing to go quietly into the night. That protest emboldened Queer communities in other cities to act in the same way. That spark lit a huge bonfire that drove the Queer community to take to the streets, to participate in acts of public protest, and to be more visible to the community and to their families.[23]

That story is well known, but other stories are less known and even more tragic. One act of incredible violence that was aimed at the Queer community and a Metropolitan Community Church congregation of gay folx is one we cannot ignore. The group was

22. Downs, *Stand By Me*, x–xi.
23. Downs, *Stand By Me*, x–xi.

targeted by hate-filled perpetrators. New Orleans, Louisiana is one of the most multicultural and diverse cities in the US. The French Quarter is a vibrant and tourist-centered area of the city. Every evening pulses with a mix of tourists, partiers, sex workers, bachelor and bachelorette partiers, musicians, outcasts, and Queer folx enjoying the flamboyance and energy of the area.

That part of New Orleans was rarely tranquil, and few would think of the French Quarter as a place to gather for church, but within the revelry that happened in that area in 1973, a small church had begun to gather every Sunday night to worship together. They gathered above the UpStairs Lounge, a gay bar in the French Quarter. On June 24, they gathered in the evening to celebrate the fourth anniversary of the Stonewall riots. In a small room upstairs from the bar, a group of about sixty to seventy people began their weekly worship. Those who gathered included some Queer folx with partners, some alone, and some with straight family members, in one instance a straight-identifying mother with her two gay sons. The church was formed because many of the Queer congregants had found no welcome in other churches, and were the victims of vitriolic language, or condemning behavior in the churches of their childhood, youth years, or as young adults. There seemed to be no safe space in established denominations and churches in the area to worship as they needed. Some still participated in the churches where they grew up but were "allowed to stay only if they kept quiet and didn't act 'too gay.'" They had been either formally or informally told they did not belong in the traditional church. Maybe someone got in their face and said, "G_d made Adam and Eve, not Adam and Steve." That night, pastor William Larson, the leader of the congregation, shared some words of hope and liberation, Followed by everyone gathering around the piano to sing with David Gary, their musician. At 7:50 PM someone or a group of unknown assailants doused the stairwell, drapes, and carpet leading to the second-floor worship space with an accelerant. For safety reasons, the steel door leading from the stairs and into the space was always kept locked. There was a speakeasy-style hatch[24] in the door

24. Speakeasies in the Roaring Twenties had to protect their patrons by

where bartenders or others would talk to a cabbie coming to drive a congregant home or let a patron enter. If they knew the person or knew someone who had called for the cabbie and the code word was uttered, they would let the person into the club. On that June night, the bartender, Buddy Rasmussen, had not called for a cab, but the buzzer sounded repeatedly. He asked one of the people in the room to open the steel fire door and to tell the cabbie he was not needed. "When he opened the door, all hell broke loose. Flames exploded into the room, and within seconds the staircase was on fire. The congregation was trapped in a barricaded bar on the edge of the French Quarter."[25] The fire was made more deadly by the bars and wooden boards that had been installed over the windows in an effort to protect the patrons and congregants from abuse they had previously experienced while in that sacred space.

That night the fire, likely perpetrated on this Queer community by hate-filled individuals, was inflicted upon those gathered there to worship a G_d who is loving and kind. Instead of that peace of worshipping a divine presence who loved them, people were forced, if they were able, to wiggle through steel bars to jump from the second floor. Some tried to breathe by poking their heads as far out of the openings as possible. In the end, thirty-two people died that night. The death count included the mother and her two gay sons who were worshipping together. Her sons, Eddie Hosea and James Curtis, died covering their mother, Mrs. Willie Inez Warren, with their bodies. Also included in the list of the deceased was Pastor Larson. Some of the attenders used fake names to protect themselves and that added to the horror that three of the men killed in the fire have never been identified.[26] For those in the Queer community in the French Quarter the fire was a genocide not seen since the witch trials of Salem and it changed many

---

keeping the police or those wishing to shut them down from entering. A small hatch where entrants had to speak a code word controlled who entered. This was a common practice for any group needing to protect those in their spaces from detection and harm.

25. Downs, *Stand By Me*, 20–21.

26. Downs, *Stand By Me*, 24.

families forever. Some families refused to pay for the funerals of their children, who they thought were straight. The fire viciously kicked them out of the "closets" where they had been living. Some victims had no way to pay medical bills since they had no health insurance. Still others never acknowledged that they were present that night and lived with the decision to remain secret for many years.[27] Reading the description of the events of that night is sobering, but so is knowing the next steps also propelled the newly emerging gay rights movement further along.

The Metropolitan Community Church, the denomination of that upstairs church in the French Quarter, was founded by Rev. Troy Perry. Shortly after the fire, the national headquarters of the denomination, which was located in Los Angeles, appealed through the media and sent several individuals to help with the response. Rev. Perry immediately left for New Orleans, where he provided comfort to the victims and their families, but he was adamant that local and national broadcasters understand that "bars" for the gay community were more than a place to drink and dance. They were community centers that provided "hope" for the persons who came there. He insisted to them that this community of faith, located over a gay bar, was indeed a church and that they belonged to a national denomination that spanned from Los Angeles to Atlanta. That place, like many across the country meeting in bars and homes, was sacred to the community. He reminded media and political leaders that this community in New Orleans, who had gathered for a "beer bust" to celebrate the anniversary of Stonewall, was just the beginning of the story. He wanted everyone to understand that truth, but he also wished for others to hear that many at that beer bust remained to worship together that Sunday evening in that upstairs worship space in New Orleans. He normalized the worshipping community at the same time he called for justice.[28]

Hosting a public memorial was problematic since many Queer people were still in the closet and that many of the friends

27. Downs, *Stand By Me,* 32.
28. Downs, *Stand By Me.*

and survivors were not willing to publicly attend. Finding a church that would allow the memorial service also proved problematic as a number of churches refused to allow the service or flat-out hung up on Perry when he called to inquire about hosting.[29] He found a church to host the event and there was a sense of relief in being together, but that gathering was fraught with danger. At the memorial service, Rev. Perry encouraged those in the Queer community in New Orleans and elsewhere to "openly embrace their spirituality and their sexuality." The service allowed those there to cry, to mourn, and to connect with other families and survivors for the first time since the fire.[30] After the memorial service was over, Rev. Perry was alerted to the presence of the media outside the church. He announced to the group that the press had arrived. He told the congregation they could exit through the back door to preserve the secrecy many lived as part of their Queer lives. He told those present that he would draw the press's attention by exiting the front to face the cameras himself. Still years later, Rev. Perry reports solemnly that every single person there walked out the front doors together. Each of them faced the cameras and for some it was their very public coming out.[31] This is a stunning moment in Queer history and the foundation of a church and denomination that continues to welcome and to be centered around communities of inclusion and full welcome.

However, I had never heard about this story until I started researching for this book. Two events inextricably bound together, at Stonewall Inn in New York City and the UpStairs Lounge in New Orleans, form part of the backbone that led the gay rights and the gay liberation movements in the US to coalesce and to become increasingly more vocal about the need to be seen *and* heard both as a community and as individuals. Other Queer-affirming churches were victims of arson over the two years after the New Orleans fire, including churches in Los Angeles, Santa Monica, Nashville,

---

29. Downs, *Stand By Me*, 32–33
30. Downs, *Stand By Me*.
31. Sears, *Rebels, Rubyfruits and Rhinestones*, 106.

and San Francisco.[32] Many in the Queer community were sick and tired of being attacked for who they were and for who they loved. For many, this event marked a "before" and "after" demarcation for their lives. Before and after Stonewall and before and after the UpStairs Lounge fire provide a reference for the beginning of that movement. Before and after are often important markers for faith traditions, as well—Christianity is marked by the before of Jesus' life and ministry and the after of his death and resurrection.

These events are not ancient history. They happened within my lifetime. I had heard of Stonewall, and it shaped my understanding of modern history of Queer lives. I heard in that story the need to fight back against social and civil authorities who were denying the dignity of Queer lives. But I had no idea how to fight. I was seven when Stonewall happened. But it would be years before I heard about that night and the nights that followed in NYC. I was sixty when I heard about the UpStairs Lounge Fire. What other stories of defiance had I missed? Probably too many to count. They are as possible in 2024 as they were in 1969 and 1973.

For me, there were no guidebooks or instruction manuals letting me know what being a lesbian looked like or even how lesbian intimacy worked. When I got to college a friend told me about the Rita Mae Brown book *Rubyfruit Jungle*, and my eyes were opened immediately. The book came out in 1973, but living in a small Texas town, I didn't have access to it. It was revolutionary and I still cannot fathom how it was published in 1973. I didn't find anything that helped me until reading that book, after finding it in an eclectic little bookstore in the town where I was attending college, and after finding a little gay bar that was heavily lesbian-oriented but really guarded by secrecy in the early eighties in West Texas. Those two things changed my life. The book also launched a more connected lesbian community, who as Rubyfruits insisted on "immediacy, confrontations, and resoluteness."[33] At times, the gay and lesbian agendas for recognition and affirmation ran counter to the others'. But one thing was happening during this period—Queer

32. Downs, *Stand By Me*, 36–37.
33. Sears, *Rebels, Rubyfruits and Rhinestones*, 3.

people of every variety were coming out. Jack Nichols and Lige Clarke were authors and editors for *Gay*, an early Queer newspaper. They described the "coming out" process in their book, *I Have More Fun*, published in 1969.

> As queer persons "we'd always known it inwardly. But now, it seemed, an ancient fact was establishing itself outwardly. What was it? That is [*sic*] love's wonderfully varied expressions *can* break through unreal crusts of fear and misunderstanding. That love *can* come out of the past's dark closets. Casting off the vile coating of social falsehood, men and women *can* bloom, standing proudly."[34]

The historical energies that were finding a footing during that time created for me and for many in the Queer community chances to be genuinely ourselves despite the undercurrents of ancient Greek and Roman understandings of sexuality or the legal and personal jeopardy our gay siblings experienced during the Nazi regime or the attacks on the UpStairs Lounge. Momentum sparked by Stonewall joined with the energy of "the sexual revolution, youthful rebellion, and third-world revolutionary movement—transformed Stonewall from a small-scale riot into a major political movement that attracted the attention of *Time, Newsweek, Look, Esquire*, and the *New York Times*."[35] These were the stories that were circling around my life. Some stories I knew, some I found in books, some I found in the conversations of hushed voices at the Oak Bar in Abilene, Texas, and some I have encountered over the forty-plus years since I graduated from high school in a little town where *gay* was the word no one dared speak.

As I shared the story of my friend Brian in chapter 1, I was naïve about AIDS and its spread. By the early eighties I was somewhat aware of the AIDS crisis on both an individual and community-wide level. When Brian shared that he had "gay cancer," I had no real idea what he was talking about. I saw periodic news stories

---

34. Sears, *Rebels, Rubyfruits and Rhinestones*, 32–33.
35. Sears, *Rebels, Rubyfruits and Rhinestones*, 30.

about it but had no clue how it would impact Brian and the rest of the world.

> An international medical crisis was threatening the lives of gay men first, and later others who contracted the "Gay Cancer," later known as HIV/AIDS (HIV—human immunodeficiency virus), which is a virus that attacks the body's immune system. If HIV is not treated, it can lead to AIDS (acquired immunodeficiency syndrome).[36]

This disease also led to either forced or medically necessitated coming out. To date over 40.1 million persons have died from AIDS and another 38 million are living with HIV/AIDS. This was and in some places still is a global crisis, and most didn't even know it existed unless they knew someone dying, which included most infected persons until the nineties. Or people heard and saw both politicians and religious leaders label those living and dying of the disease as getting their due justice for living an immoral and abhorrent life.

My friend Brian did not show signs of the disease for months, then he showed up at work wearing long sleeves and gloves in the sweltering heat of August in West Texas. He had begun showing lesions on the skin that he failed badly at hiding as they progressed. He could no longer stay closeted as a gay man or as an AIDS patient. These symptoms were new, but he had endured a persistent cough, nausea, exhaustion, swollen lymph nodes, and abdominal issues for several months. We talked about his illness, but not about the specifics. Maybe deep down, I didn't want to know his chances of surviving the disease. I took him meals and watched old movies with him as his strength level meant he was unable to leave the house anymore. Other friends and family began to distance themselves from him. Even his gay friends were too anxious to be near him. They knew the risks as they saw the disease spread throughout the gay community. They had friends dying right and

---

36. Center for Disease Control, https://www.cdc.gov/hiv/basics/whatishiv. html. Additional information can be found on the World Health Organization's website related to HIV/AIDS, https://www.cdc.gov/hiv/basics/whatishiv. html.

left. I didn't understand it all. I hoped he would recover, but I was afraid. He knew the statistics and the death process he had seen in others, and I did not. As I shared in chapter 1, I visited several times and was required to wear head-to-foot protective gear to enter his room, which had a sign out front for no one to enter without permission of medical personnel. Medical personnel on his floor were few and often I didn't see anyone on the floor at all. His room was on a previously unused floor with another ten "gay cancer," HIV/AIDS, patients. He was isolated on multiple levels. Near the end, I once again donned the required protective gear[37] and went to his room to read to him, but he was gone. No one had called to tell me I needed to come to say goodbye. I was heartbroken and angry with those who had deserted him.

The sign on his door told folx to avoid him unless they absolutely had a medical reason to enter. We must remember our Queer siblings, labeled with a pink triangle, who were killed in Nazi gas chambers or by firing squad. These words and acts of condemnation against homosexual behavior have been happening for centuries and they continue into the evangelical church of the twentieth and twenty-first centuries. Examples of this are found in the words and work of persons like Anita Bryant, Pat Robertson, and other evangelical Christian leaders. They preached a literal understanding of Scripture that led many to place that "do not enter" sign around all Queer persons. Protests against the Queer community also included signs that proclaimed, "Gay is Godless," "Keep America Beautiful. Shoot a Faggot," and others.[38] As religious leaders and pundits with wide audiences, they targeted the LGBTQIA+ community. But they weren't the only voices.

Just as Rev. Troy Perry showed up in New Orleans after the UpStairs Lounge Fire, others began to desire a counter-narrative to those being broadcast on private and public television stations.

---

37. The COVID pandemic brought back so many memories of laughter, connection, and pain in those weeks that Brian was hospitalized and dying. Wearing PPE (personal protective equipment) was required then and again when visiting several members of my congregation during the pandemic.

38. Sears, *Rebels, Rubyfruits and Rhinestones*, 265.

There was a community of gay and gay-affirming Christians who saw a need for a gay religious movement. Part of this was to counter the constant repetition of eternal damnation from the Right and silence from the Left. Part of it was to find a safe place to experience the grace and love of G_d. A part of it needed to address the texts of the Hebrew Torah and the Christian Bible passages that brought about that damnation and rejection by religious communities.

What does the Queer community—varied and diverse—want to have in their lives to live fully and authentically? What has been denied throughout ancient and modern history to the Queer community? It's actually pretty simple. Broadly the Queer community desires to:

- live an authentic life;
- have increased self-awareness and insight;
- feel free to create flexible rules for what gender means and how it is expressed;
- experience strong emotional connections with others and create supportive families of choice;
- explore new expressions of sexuality and create relationships with "new rules";
- have a unique perspective on life and with empathy and compassion for others;
- be a positive role model, mentor, and activist working for social justice;
- belong to an LGBTIAA+ community.[39]

Reexamining the ways anti-gay beliefs have emerged throughout history in a more wholistic and contextual manner can lead us to this desired reality. More on these desires in the chapters to come. These basic desires are not that different from others. We have work to do, my friends. Dismantling Queer prejudice, marginalization, and condemnation requires us to look further at the texts

39. Riggle and Rostosky, *Positive View of LGBTQ*, 4.

of the Hebrew and Christian traditions that have reinforced these feelings.

Chapter Three

Tackling the Clobber Passages

FOR THE PAST TWENTY years, I have been doing a presentation on the "clobber passages" of the Bible, which have been used for centuries to judge and condemn Queer persons. I've presented on them at church adult forums, pastoral gatherings, seminary classrooms, and at various conferences. In those presentations and talks, I have challenged the traditional understanding of these texts by utilizing historical, cultural, and critical exegesis. I challenged what I believe is centuries of condemnation using a flawed interpretation of those texts. I learned the wisdom of interpreting and challenging texts in the church that raised me, and the church that eventually caused me to leave because of my Queer life and the announcement of my marriage to my long-term partner, Cindy. When I grew up in the United Methodist Church there was a clear instruction for engaging the Bible. The acronym taught to me was STER: Scripture, tradition, experience, and reason. It is lovingly called the Wesleyan Quadrilateral,[1] even though John Wesley, the founder of the denomination, never used it in his preaching or writing. It was a process taught in my youth and later in my courses at a United Methodist seminary, Saint Paul School of Theology in Kansas City. That lesson always instructs us to begin with Scripture, because that is the foundation of living out our faith lives. But

1. Outler, ed., *John Wesley*, iv.

there are three other lenses by which we are called to view those sacred texts. One way to be more intentional in our reading is to both honor and critique the traditions of the church and how the texts are viewed and utilized. However, it does not stop there. We are then challenged to use our reason and our own experience to guide us in taking meaning from those readings. My experience was that the Divine Being we worship loves all, creates all as good, and embraces all who are sacred creations of the Creator. This process is used in the faith that brought me up to see the primacy of Scripture, but we were also challenged that Scripture never stands alone. I was reasoning and experiencing something altogether different in my understanding of the Scriptures than what would be presented at the General Conference in 1972, which inserted in a petition brought to the organizing body of the denomination. It stated "that homosexuality is not compatible with Christian teaching" and that any "self-avowed, practicing homosexual, could not be ordained in the church."[2]

Growing up in West Texas, I knew fundamentalist and evangelical Christians. I thought they were the same thing and that they were all inherently anti-gay. What I learned later was that evangelicals come from the "right, left and middle regarding political and cultural issues. Fundamentalism is more monolithic politically and more conservative theologically than evangelicalism."[3] The piece of fundamentalism that triggers caution for me and other political and theological progressives is their insistence on the doctrine of the inerrancy of the Bible. For some that means the Bible is primary and is absolute truth. These folx say "No, Period" to other possible interpretations. For many "inerrancy holds that the Bible gives accurate and up-to-the-minute information, not only on religious matters, but on all things that the Bible addresses, including science and history. It encourages a literal reading of Scripture."[4] This is where things get tricky. As a Methodist I learned to use all the elements of STER in reading and interpreting texts.

2. UMC *Book of Discipline,* ¶ 304.3, Qualifications for Ordination.

3. Rogers, *Jesus, the Bible, and Homosexuality,* 7.

4. Rogers, *Jesus, the Bible, and Homosexuality,* 7.

Fundamentalism in the South was and is a dominating force that is growing across the country. But I saw people in my life and on the peripheral of my family and friends who wore clothing of different textures, wore jewelry, shaved sideburns, and ate animals not considered appropriate in the biblical texts.[5] There are 613 laws/commandments in the Hebrew Bible. These laws are fundamental to the lifeblood of our Jewish siblings. For most Christians these laws seem archaic and not in line with their own understanding of a relationship with G_d. Many of these laws are problematic from a modern perspective due to the specificity of the laws for a time very removed from our own. Jesus' life, death, and resurrection fulfilled the law. Christians have never been under the law of the Old Testament, which makes it even more problematic when someone cherry-picks laws from it that they want enforced and others they would choose to forget altogether. I believe this type of judgment is based on a misreading of the message they see in the clobber texts. The result of clinging to the adherence to the laws of a testament, which we use primarily for narrativity of the human story, makes everything even more messy in the relationship between the church and the Queer community.

From my experience far too many ignored these "annoying" commandments and focused all of their judgment on women, on other races, and on those they deem especially sinful, the Queer community. They do these things through their inerrant understanding of Scripture. That was the opinion in my small community in West Texas. Even though my dad preached about love and the grace of G_d, the community we lived in was deeply connected to Southern Baptist faith, fundamentalism, and Roman Catholic beliefs around many issues important to me and my faith. In that geographic place, I was both a young woman and a lesbian, both considered less-than and/or sinful. I knew I was different as a child but had no words for it. I knew it as a youth trying to find a place where I belonged. I knew it when my church and I were picketed by the Westboro Baptist Church with their hate-filled signs. And I

5. Levitical laws forbid these things, but they are seldom enforced in the majority of Christian traditions.

know it now. Still there are people in the fundamentalist and right-leaning evangelical movements that view me as damaged goods due to a perceived "choice" I made at some point in my life about my sexuality. They use this language to marginalize me and my siblings in the Queer community.

Thus, the battle lines are drawn, and war is waged by those who read the Bible as a literal and inerrant document and those who use a hermeneutic, like the STER hermeneutic I was taught in the UMC, to help guide me in my reading and interpretation of the Bible. Both sides of the biblical interpretation scale and those in between share one thing in common. They are reading the biblical text to add meaning and direction in how to live out their understanding of faith and discipleship. Regardless of that common behavior, we come to very different understandings of what G_d, through the interpretation of biblical texts, is telling us about our siblings.

These two Western perspectives, a progressive and liberal interpretation of the text and the fundamentalist inerrant and literal reading, can lead to a significant misunderstanding of Scripture. However, it is not as dualistic or as binary as we often think. There is a spectrum by which individuals interpret the biblical text. I share these potential perspectives with those in my workshops on the Bible and interpretation.

- The Bible is the literal and infallible word of G_d written through human hands.
- The Bible is inspired by G_d but is fallible.
- The Bible is helpful to bring people to faith and salvation in Jesus Christ.
- The Bible is a good book that inspires people to live better lives.

E. Randolph Richards and Brandon J. O'Brien, in *Misreading Scripture with Western Eyes: Removing Cultural Blinders to Better Understand the Bible*, lay out the quandary for modern Christians. The biblical text was written thousands of years ago in a culture and time with mores and traditions that are quite different than ours. Even modern Christians with their own learned mores and traditions often clash with other Western cultures. Because of these significant differences there is the possibility, maybe even the inevitability, of clashing mores and traditions. Many times, these differing positions are a "given" in one culture and not appropriate in another.[6] Attitudes and expectations in my small West Texas upbringing are very different than those I encounter in the urban Philadelphia environment where I now live and where our son has spent the bulk of his adolescent and young adult years. His downtown school, The Creative and Performing Arts High School, was filled with artists, musicians, poets, writers, dancers, and actors, many of whom consider themselves gender-fluid and most of whom are completely affirming of anyone else's sexuality, gender, gender identity, gender expression, or any other emerging identities they claim. The shifting perspectives of the modern world are creating opportunities for Queer folk to be affirmed in their homes and in their schools. This would have been inconceivable to my fifteen-year-old self. I sometimes wonder how my life would have been different with that kind of affirmation. I'll never know, but that question has made me even more committed to create spaces for all Queer kids out there.

The changing and concretized beliefs and mores in our contexts means that we approach the texts of our faith often with completely affirming or opposing interpretative lens. Or they lie somewhere in between. This leads to another problematic issue—the dualistic Western view of things being "true or false, right or wrong, good or bad."[7] Ambiguity becomes, for many in the Western world, a "dirty word." Using the lesson I learned from my parents—things were either true or false, good or evil, right or wrong.[8] When I found my life to be somewhere in the middle, I

6. Richards and O'Brien, *Misreading Scripture with Western Eyes*, 32.

7. Richards and O'Brien, *Misreading Scripture with Western Eyes*, 33.

8. A problematic duality as the term equates white as good and black as bad all too often. Allyship with my siblings of color means I no longer utilize this analogy, but it definitely was evident in my household growing up.

was incapable of discerning a way out of the darkness. There was no guideline or owner's manual to lead me out. And that puts us smack dab in the middle of a mess. Shifting mores, traditions, and difficult dualities when reading a text common to Christians all over the globe means we read the text and discern very different intent in the words of our Savior, Jesus Christ, as recorded in the Gospels and the Pauline letters that form our faith story. They also lead to increasingly complex conversations about those texts.

Another issue raised by Richards and O'Brien relates to language as a vital part of discussing our faith, our personal lives, a family adventure, or the death of a loved one. We utilize words that are often common when we speak within our own cultural context. We often run into inadequate word usage. How do you describe the mountains from the perspective of the Poconos to a person whose only experience with mountain ranges is the Swiss Alps? How do you say "I love you" to a Sunday school student who has just offered you a gift for Pastor Appreciation Month and then say those same words to your beloved spouse who has been their partner for over sixty years? Words mean different things in cultures far and wide, and in highly divergent circumstances. In the English-speaking world, we have one word that is used for several different types of love. However, biblical texts show us that "Greek has at least four words for love: agape, philia, eros, and storge."[9] Universal and selfless love is called *agape*. *Philia* is affectionate love and is the root of the slogan of the city where I live and work— Philadelphia: The City of Brotherly Love and Sisterly Affection (the second part is important to me but has not caught on with all Philadelphians). *Eros* is the word for love that is romantic and passionate. Finally, familial love is *storge* love. Language is complicated. And that is also true in the Hebrew, Aramaic, and Greek words used in the creation of the Bible. The nuances of language as the Bible was written, as it was and is translated in many different interpretative versions, and as we read those words today have different values, meanings, and mores.[10]

9. Richards and O'Brien, *Misreading Scripture with Western Eyes*, 73.

10. Richards and O'Brien, *Misreading Scripture with Western Eyes*, 73.

This understanding is one part of the challenge we face in preaching when looking at centuries-old texts in a context unknown to them or their cultural and religious worldviews. We can try to bend and make those words relevant for today but the further we stretch their "meaning" the harder that task is. When people make their own experiences and opinions the inerrant framework, by which they read and interpret Scripture, we are all then entering into a dangerous place, fraught with jeopardy for those who are chosen to judge based on that personal framework.

We venture into murky and dangerous waters when we take on the "clobber passages" of the Hebrew Bible and the New Testament. I have been using that phrase for over a decade and have no memory where I got it. However, Jacob. D. Myers has provided a guide in his book, *Making Love with Scripture: Why the Bible Doesn't Mean How You Think It Means*. The first premise to learn is that we cannot interpret the Bible outside of ourselves. I am a white, cisgender[11] lesbian who often lives into a nonbinary gender expression. I have three advanced degrees, several of which I am still paying the student loans I incurred getting those degrees for. I am a professor and a pastor, and I was raised by two people who also had advanced degrees. I am an American with a place to live, work, shop, and thrive without military conflict on land or in the sky. I am decidedly middle class with enough money to do some of the things I want to, but not enough to do some of the things I dream of doing. I have a pension that is more than many and not as much as I likely will need. I walk into any physical or digital space with all of that. I cannot leave that identity outside for a while to interpret the biblical text. It is mostly who I am and who I know myself to be. But even that knowledge about self can change with new insights, fresh learnings, and lived experiences. Who I am on multiple levels flavors and directly impacts how I think, how I make decisions, what causes I support, who I include as "chosen family," how I express my gender, and how I view the world around

11. I identify with the gender that was assigned at my birth; however, my gender expression is nonbinary. That expression comes out in my choices of clothing, footwear, hairstyle, and mannerisms.

me. That brings me back to Scripture being primary, but always being interpreted using tradition, reason, and experience.

We now turn to the "clobber passages" of the Hebrew Bible and the New Testament that have been used over centuries to beat down, or "clobber," the Queer community, who are judged negatively using these texts in their literal and infallible ways of interpretation. While I won't go into intricate detail on all the clobber texts, I start with the one most well-known of the Hebrew Bible "clobber passages." The first of the texts that are used against the Queer community is Genesis 19:1–11.

> The two angels came to Sodom in the evening, and Lot was sitting in the gateway of Sodom. When Lot saw them, he rose to meet them and bowed down with his face to the ground. He said, "Please, my lords, turn aside to your servant's house and spend the night and wash your feet; then you can rise early and go on your way." They said, "No; we will spend the night in the square." But he urged them strongly, so they turned aside to him and entered his house, and he made them a feast and baked unleavened bread, and they ate. But before they lay down, the men of the city, the men of Sodom, both young and old, all the people to the last man, surrounded the house, and they called to Lot, "Where are the men who came to you tonight? Bring them out to us, so that we may know them." Lot went out of the door to the men, shut the door after him, and said, "I beg you, my brothers, do not act so wickedly. Look, I have two daughters who have not known a man; let me bring them out to you, and do to them as you please; only do nothing to these men, for they have come under the shelter of my roof." But they replied, "Stand back!" And they said, "This fellow came here as an alien, and he would play the judge! Now we will deal worse with you than with them." Then they pressed hard against the man Lot and came near the door to break it down. But the men inside reached out their hands and brought Lot into the house with them and shut the door. And they struck with blindness the

men who were at the door of the house, both small and great, so that they were unable to find the door.[12]

The interpretation of this text has for millennia held that it was the sin of homosexuality that led to the destruction of Sodom and Gomorrah by G_d. The text baffled me as a youth for the first time in a friend's church where I was visiting as the preacher from the pulpit condemned all "gay and lesbian persons who were named unnatural and wholly repugnant before the Lord." At the same time that I was learning to understand my own sexuality, I was besieged by internal questions, "Is this what G_d will do to me?" "Am I doomed to fire and destruction?" "Is this really who I am destined to be?" "Would G_d really do this . . . again?" These questions lingered for years. I just took the story as one more way that Queer people are marginalized and condemned. That definitely included me. It brought a sense of doom to me. I didn't question the text as much as I did later when I questioned the ways people were interpreting the text to exclude me and my Queer siblings. Asking those questions then and today is part of the journey of self-awareness and self-love. When I went to seminary at the age of thirty-one, I finally learned to really look at that text from all the lens of interpretation. That's a lot of years believing the myth of Sodom and Gomorrah and awaiting my impending fire, damnation, and doom. And a long time for my Queer siblings to be subjected to this kind of judgment.

Genesis chapters 18 and 19 have a similar structure. A man of G_d, Abraham first and then Lot, welcome divine visitors. They welcome them wholeheartedly with food and drink. Their hospitality is seen as living into the call and laws of Jewish faith, to welcome the stranger. Abraham is blessed by the visit, which also included the Lord. He is told of the destruction of Sodom and Gomorrah. "The storyteller wants us to know that whatever is going on in Sodom and Gomorrah is so corrupt, so horrendous, so *not* moral and just, that it gets the attention of the God-who-hears-the-cries-of-the-oppressed. Future generations are meant

12. Genesis 19:1–11, NRSV. The story continues, through verse 29, with G_d destroying Sodom and Gomorrah.

to be reminded of these contrasting postures."[13] Lot is blessed by the visitors and shares fellowship with them. But the story takes a hugely problematic turn. All of the men of Sodom, yes all of them, arrive at his house, decidedly unhospitable. They demand Lot turn his visitors over to them. Lot does all he can to protect his visitors, even offering up his virginal daughters, an act that is problematic on every level, but is too often ignored in the use of the story to clobber the Queer community. If the men of Sodom are indeed homosexual, why offer them women in the first place? The act of dominating and controlling these foreigners is about power, not sex. They refuse to listen to Lot, who is a foreigner himself having only lived there about twenty years. He escapes with his wife and two daughters, but we all know "the rest of the story" about Lot's wife disobeying G_d's messenger to not turn back and when she does she is turned into a pillar of salt. Genesis 18 is about hospitality. Genesis 19 is about inhospitality and how depraved people can become with blinders on about who they define as "other."[14]

I am clear that this brutal behavior had nothing to do with mature, responsible, and loving same-sex attraction and relationships. There was no understanding at that time about the idea of sexual orientation. The story is about power and control over men they deemed foreign "scum," who they could and wanted to abuse. It is about the failure to be hospitable to strangers. In the Bible, Sodom represented evil. Using the mythology of Sodom and Gomorrah as a rationale for clobbering and demeaning the Queer community is nothing more than a poorly exegeted biblical framework, used to base hatred and exclusion upon.

Finally, another question must be asked about the story of Sodom and Gomorrah. Why was this one of the few stories retold generation after generation and preserved in Scripture? And why continue to adhere to a false interpretation to clobber Queer folx? For Colby Martin and others, the answer is in the Bible itself. Both the Hebrew Bible and the New Testament counter the interpretation of sexual immorality being the crux of the text. To ignore

13. Martin, *Unclobber*, 51–52.
14. Martin, *Unclobber*, 52–56.

the teachings of Hebrew leaders like Isaiah, Ezekiel, Jeremiah, and biblical scholars *and* to also refuse to hear even Jesus' own words.

> What if we learned from our misuse of this Clobber Passage and instead took to heart the real message of Sodom and Gomorrah? Historically this passage has been seen as evidence for a God who opposes homosexuality so ardently that God would destroy entire cities as a result. It has been a story used to separate the LGBTQ community from the rest of the flock, to keep them as outsiders. And yet, when understood properly, the entire point of Genesis 19 is that the people of God are called to be people who receive the outcast and the outsiders, not create them.[15]

As both a pastor and a professor, I am often asked about this passage and others regarding my own sexuality and my public witness about Queer lives mattering. My response about the role of Scripture to suppress Queer representation, presence, and leadership is echoed in the above quote. We are as children of G_d required, challenged, and called to be open and affirming of G_d's children and our siblings. G_d's word and the example of Jesus' life and ministry is to see an expansive and ever-inclusive vision of the community of G_d. Misreading a text that has been shown repeatedly to be misinterpreted just inflicts more pain on the Queer community.

I am convicted on one thing about biblical interpretation—the context matters. The subject of not being hospitable from Genesis 19 and other contextual nuances from the social structure help readers see new interpretative opportunities for the clobber passages. Any passage that we look at related to anti-homosexual thinking would be inaccurate in how Christians should hear them. Jesus should be our interpretative lens and we are challenged to see these texts through the life, ministry, and teachings of Jesus Christ. However, Jesus never uttered a word, as far as we know, that condemned persons for same-sex sexual immorality or for being Queer. Not one word.

15. Martin, *Unclobber,* 60.

We turn next to the writing of the apostle Paul. I need to admit from the start that I have a love/hate relationship with him (okay it's probably disgust more than hate), which too often leans toward hate. His writings about women, that are contradicted by other writings supposedly penned by Paul or his followers, and other theological contradictions give me more than pause.[16] We are all reflections of the divine. The image for generations has been a G_d desiring one man and one woman committed to each other. After all, Adam and Eve are the standard and that fact comes from heteronormative cultural bias. Insisting on that specific image of G_d leads us away from the actual biblical text. "Biblically Jesus Christ is the image of God (Col 1:15; Cor 4:4). But the image of God in Jesus was not the consequence of some unique human attribute, like maleness or marital status. It was rather the result of his reflecting the love of God fully in his life."[17]

The second passage I want to address is Romans 1:26–27. As we delve into this text there are two problematic assumptions to be aware of—first, that gender is simply binary (which I firmly denounce) and second, that the activity of mature homosexual relationships is being addressed in these verses (also denounced by me through my scholarship, life experiences, and faith formation). The text reads as follows:

> For this reason God gave them up to degrading passions. Their women exchanged natural intercourse for unnatural, and in the same way also the men, giving up natural intercourse with women, were consumed with passion for one another. Men committed shameless acts with men and received in their own persons the due penalty for their error.[18]

---

16. The differences can be traced to the conflict some scholars still share in regard to which epistles Paul wrote and those written by his followers in his style of writing. Romans from an academic standpoint was written by Paul to the church at Rome.

17. Rogers, *Jesus, the Bible, and Homosexuality*, 88.

18. Romans 1:26–27, NRSV.

Three thousand verses from the Bible share insights into how we are to love our neighbors and the call to take care of the poor, and those who have been left on the side of the road like the victim cared for by the good Samaritan.[19] These are primary in our understanding of how we are to live in the world as people of faith. There are only a handful of texts that have been misinterpreted, taken out of context, and used to condemn homosexuality. None of these texts, if interpreted closely using more modern skills of reading the texts and contexts through the life of Jesus and the STER paradigm I learned as a United Methodist, are addressing the Queer community of the twenty-first century.[20] To use them this way is to use the Bible as a weapon. If we weaponize the Scriptures, then we do injustice, not only to our Queer siblings who have experienced repeated trauma both directly and/or indirectly, but to other marginalized persons, and we betray our baptismal vows.

My love/hate relationship with Paul comes into sharp focus in the letter he wrote to the church in Rome. It was a diverse group of both gentiles and Jewish-Christians. Paul was writing after the Jews of Rome had been expelled from the city during the rule of Emperor Claudius. He had thrown out Jewish-Christian converts due to their protests to bring the teachings of Jesus into their world. When Claudius died, the edict was ended. This was when Jewish-Christians returned. The divided church they were returning to and the frustrations of community led to Paul's letter to the house church in Rome.[21] Romans is a complicated book. Some view it as a full summation of Paul's theology. It is instead a letter written to a particular people, at a particular moment in time, at a particular geographic location, and to address particular issues arising in the churches there. I contend that you cannot use Romans as an unerring metric to determine faith and limited morality expectations of our times. That's just not what the letter is about.

Paul wrote to the church in Rome to address the gentile Jesus-following community to explain the mission of Jesus in a way they

---

19. Rogers, *Jesus, the Bible, and Homosexuality*, 89.
20. Rogers, *Jesus, the Bible, and Homosexuality*, 88.
21. Martin, *Unclobber*, 117.

would understand. The church at Rome was a divided community. They were divided along ethnic lines. Paul wanted to stave off any threat to the universally inclusive message of salvation through Jesus Christ, who came for all the earth.[22] It is that message from Paul that gives me hope and allows me to see grace more clearly. But we see a change in his tune pretty quickly in Romans 1:26–27. This was one of the passages that my roommate freshman year quoted to me daily as she sought to "save my soul from eternal damnation." Luckily that roommate didn't last long, and I had a private room for the rest of the academic year. And it was in that personal space that I began to find my identity as a lesbian and to hear my own voice. I read *Rubyfruit Jungle*, had my first sexual experience with a woman, and wrestled with the Hebrew Bible and Paul while attending a small United Methodist college in Abilene, Texas. It's a religious college and intro to religion was required. In that class I heard the professor and other students talk about "those people" and "the gays." It was also in that class where I first heard a lone student ask the question, "Why does Paul hate gay people so much?" The answer my religion professor gave broke me inside. He said that G_d wants us to "love the sinner but not the sin," which clearly says Queer folks are perverted sinners. Lord, have I heard that phrase a lot. If I had a nickel . . . well, you know that line. I transferred to Texas Tech the next semester and never looked back.

Paul was writing to a specific context with a specific need. That need was for Paul to stop the fracturing of the Roman church community around ethnicity issues. He also wanted to make a larger point in Romans 1:18–32 using a rhetorical device, which Aristotle called epideictic discourse, to have his readers heap blame on one group to then rally them to an understanding of shared hatred of a specific group to create a common enemy. This rhetorical device can also be used to praise or affirm a group.[23] These verses were by design "to heap blame on the wicked and

---

22. Martin, *Unclobber*, 117–18.
23. Martin, *Unclobber*, 121–22.

ungodly people that this passage was describing."[24] This likely was the reasoning behind putting the text in his correspondence to that community.

A partial bit of grace that I found in my dorm room was the very next verse, Romans 2:1, which declares that there is no excuse to condemn others. The judgment of the behavior condemned in Romans 1:18–32 is G_d's responsibility, not ours. Judging others leads to our own condemnation. That college roommate was denying G_d's word through Christ Jesus of inclusion, love, and grace. Instead, her focus was on everything she "hated" about my very being from what she had been taught about those few verses in Romans. She had heard teaching on these texts in her evangelical church through preaching that constantly denigrated "the gays" with judgment and condemnation. She had been carefully taught to hate the Queer community and to fear them since the behaviors described in Romans 1, and elsewhere, were clearly defined and inerrant. Trying to preach on this text or other "clobber passages" is a struggle if you don't understand the context and purpose of their writing. Some choose to avoid that hard and intentional work due to their own fears of conflict or questioning. Coming into that environment with care and intentionality is required. So many people have heard the text as one of terror—for those scared of an agenda of recruitment of gay converts (as if that is how Queer people are created) into the Queer community or for those who are Queer, whether they were living into that identity or not. In a paper I wrote for *Between Text and Sermon*, I shared the following:

> Spending significant time on the particularities of this text brings a plethora of options, and most of these options lead to places that are problematic for preaching. The "females" addressed in the text could be having intercourse with each other or some variation of unnatural sexual behavior with men.[25]

24. Martin, *Unclobber*, 122.

25. Murphy, "More Evidence Pertaining to 'Their Females' in Romans 1:26."

The men's sexual behavior with other men in vs. 27 and
what it represented has been hotly debated through
much of the history of biblical interpretation. There
is hardly consensus on the subject. The question of
whether Paul was condemning homoerotic behavior
in general, Greco-Roman pederasty (the practice of an
adult male using a minor male for sexual gratification),
or the condemnation of excessive sexual passion within
the community almost seems beside the point.[26]

It is crucial to understand that these two verses are part of
a larger section where Paul's purpose was to bring together a diverse and conflicted group of gentiles and Jews following Jesus in
Rome by consolidating against an enemy for the church, a focus
that would hopefully result in unity. The verses are extremely
similar to the words in the Wisdom of Solomon. The goal of that
book "was, in part, to strengthen the divide between the Jews and
Gentiles; to remind the Jewish people that G_d was *for* them and
against the pagan nations."[27] Perpetuating the us vs. them motif
in the Jewish people was alive and well in the first-century world.
Paul was using the beliefs of Jews that are to our modern ears full
of prejudice and manipulation in an attempt to quell discord in
the community. Bullies use similar methodology. They attempt to
isolate their target, sow negative opinions about their victims, and
then to use the uproar caused to legitimize or to gain additional
persons to their "side." Many Queer folx have been on the receiving end of this kind of behavior. First bullies use name-calling to
sever the bond to others in earshot of their hateful language, then
to gain supporters who will empower the bully to continue their
behavior or to protect the bully, and lastly to help in the isolation
and rejection of the abused party. I cannot even begin to count the
number of times I was on the receiving end of this kind of name-
calling and bullying. This Queer kid always walked into school, the
church, and public spaces with their guard up. I still do in some
spaces. Being called a faggot, dyke, lesbo, or something similar

26. Kuhn, "Natural and Unnatural Relations Between Text and Context."
27. Martin, *Unclobber*, 122.

has been a frequent part of my life—especially during my younger years. A popular meme on Facebook states the following: "Queer people don't grow up as ourselves, we grow up playing a version of ourselves that sacrifices authenticity to minimize humiliation and prejudice. The massive task of our adult lives is to unpick which parts of ourselves are truly us and which parts we've created to protect us."[28] If the Bible is used to contribute to that humiliation and abuse, there is no wonder why many in the Queer community choose to stay clear of the institutional church.

What do we do with this dilemma of utilizing religious texts to exclude and diminish the Queer community? How do we enter the sanctuary or step into the pulpit and combat the misrepresentation of Scripture to hurting people? How do we begin to heal the repeated trauma the church has inflicted on our Queer siblings, and how can we help this to come about by beginning to see them fully and to apologize for that trauma even if we do not think we have been part of that trauma? How do we re-engage those who have left the church and religion altogether because of these hurtful verses used out of context? Can we reach those marginalized by the use of these clobber passages at all? What does preaching look like that takes seriously the needs of a church to recover from the infliction of pain on so many siblings? Tackling the theology imbedded in the condemnation of the Queer community is deeply needed.

28. Facebook meme. See https://www.advocate.com/media/2020/1/08/tweet-struggle-growing-queer-goes-viral.

Chapter Four

Can We Find
a "Yes, PERIOD" Theology?

I BELIEVE THAT EVERYONE has some level of theological insight.
They just might not know it. They might understand it as a "worldview" or an underlying "foundation" of how they live and interact
in the world. They might see it as an ethical or moralistic way to
view everything around them. The word *theology* might be scary
or foreign to them. The word *theology* literally means thinking
about G_d. Some folx have a theology or mindset of doubt or
outright disbelief in G_d when they ponder the possibility of the
great unknown in their lives. They may have never experienced
G_d or they have been turned away from the church and their
beliefs through abuse, traumatic teachings, or by being thrown
out of their church for being true to who G_d actually made
them to be. Or maybe they grew up in a home where faith was
not present. Others have a well-developed and broad theology of
inclusion and grace when thinking about G_d. These folx have
been nurtured into faith in their youth or as an adult by hearing
sermons and teachings that affirm the sacred worth of all persons
(y'all means all—from my Texas roots). Still others have a deeply
entrenched theology of G_d that excludes and casts judgment on
other beloved creations, ones they perceive as being trapped in a
sinful existence of their own choosing. This type of theology has

been part of the struggle during the Queer march for basic human rights and dignity, either by acts perpetrated toward their authentic selves or by the church that professes this theology of exclusion and judgment. They would not describe their expression of faith and their understanding of G_d in these negative ways. I believe they would define their beliefs around the Queer community as trying to "love the sinner NOT the sin," "saving one of G_d's [also they would not use this way to write the name of G_d] lost children," or "they are perverts, abusers, and they are trying to recruit others into being gay." All of those are inaccurate and downright offensive descriptions. However, not all of this is based in faith. Ludger Viefhues-Bailey writes that politics plays a significant role in the ways conservatives view homosexuality. Part of his research states that we need to address the topic in this way.

> What conservative Christians say about same-sex love [needs to begin] by asking what motivates this discourse. This seems to be an easy question. Is it not apparent that conservative Christians base their beliefs on a literal reading of the Bible? And if it is not the Bible that motivates them, then it must be that conservative politics (and not deep-seated religious convictions) determine how conservative Christians think about same-sex love.[1]

The reality is people are shaped and formed by the theology or lack of theology in their homes and lives during very important formative years. There has been an almost constant level of anti-Queer hatred that the media and conservative religious teachings have perpetuated for as long as the church and culture have been present on the earth. There have been political leanings taught by word or example by those around them, as was my experience.

The theology of G_d I had as a child and probably into my youth was an image of an old, white man in white robes with long gray-white hair and a long beard sitting on a great throne in the clouds. I may not have known it at the time but due to the heteronormative reality both in culture and in the church, I likely saw G_d as straight, although that might have been only subconsciously. Why

---

1. Viefhues-Bailey, "Religious Interests Between Bible and Politics."

did I see and understand G_d in that way? Those were the images that I heard described. The Cokesbury Sunday school curriculum showed G_d that way. I'm sure the religious movies and TV shows perpetuated that image as well, until I saw George Burns and later Morgan Freeman play the role of G_d on screen in the movies *Oh, God!* and *Bruce Almighty*. But I certainly didn't consciously think about things in that way. A more expansive teaching and learning emerged as I came out and worked to define who I was in my body, my mind, my soul, and in my understanding of the world. That led me to question the image I had of the divine, but it didn't displace the theology of exclusion that I witnessed and lived within the church. Part of that exclusion was seeing the absence of anyone like me in the congregations I participated in. Part of that was hearing about backlash toward the Queer community in the 1970s and 1980s as the gay rights movement was shown on network news, even as it was often reported in a negative manner. There were clear signs that someone like me did not really belong in the church. There were no voices that I heard during my youth and into my young adult life that spoke of true welcome and affirmation in the church. If I had heard a preacher, any preacher, or even my own father speak a word of acceptance during their sermons or prayers, it might have changed things significantly. I don't blame my dad, as he had no experience of the need for a Queer-affirming message, and even if he did, the language in the 1972 UMC *Discipline* clearly named Queer folx as "incompatible with Christian teachings."[2] I felt outside of the kindom[3] of G_d. I was not welcome and was incompatible with G_d's design and intention. That led me to understand my place in the world and to learn that that place was not with G_d.

Because of these lessons, spoken and unspoken, I grew up hiding who I was because who I was to the core of my being was a sin against G_d and the church. My very being was deemed less

---

2. UMC *Book of Discipline*, ¶ 304.3 Qualifications for Ordination.

3. Kindom used in place of the kingdom is used to convey non-gendered images and descriptive language for G_d and for the community of faithful disciples aware of the need for change and inclusion.

than, or spoken about with hate, or physically removed from the places where we worked and from the communities of faith who may have reared us but turned their backs when they found out who we truly are. I doubt that there is a Queer person who hasn't experienced some form of resistance, marginalization, oppression, or abuse. The question that comes from this is "where did those who perpetrate those realities learn that theology/worldview?" Where did those folx first hear and learn that exclusive and hateful behavior toward the Queer community was okay? Where did they first hear and learn the words *Queer, fag, faggot, dyke, tranny,* or *sissy*? They heard them from their parents, friends, or mass media—TV, movies, news broadcasters, and so many others. The hate that comes from those examples of name-calling can be life-changing for a Queer kid. The names do hurt just as much as sticks and stones when they are directed at you. Statistics show that one positive and affirming adult in a Queer kid's life significantly reduces the possibility of that kid committing suicide. According to The Trevor Project, a Queer advocacy organization, "1.8 million LGBTQ youth (13–24) seriously consider suicide each year in the US—and at least one attempts suicide every 45 seconds."[4] That is stunning information. I never seriously considered that option but I know of so many of my Queer friends who either thought about it or had created a plan for committing suicide. This theology literally kills. Instead of "No, period" we need to bring a theology of "Yes, Period!" Yes, you are lovely, special, and adored. Period. But that's not what many Queer folx hear.

Unfortunately, exclusive language and condemning behavior is found in cultural, religious, and biblical understandings that cause abuse and marginalization. Some words hurt more than others. As I wrote in chapter 2, the word *Queer,* among a few other derogatory names, has been reclaimed to some extent. But we still hear "gay agenda" or "sexual preference" used to dismiss our needs, our relationships, and our lives. We still had to fight for the right to marry and the right to form our families in some nontraditional ways. It is still legal in many states to deny housing

4. The Trevor Project, "Top-line Statistics."

or job protections for the Queer community. I received a note in 2022 from a member of my church that said, "We really enjoy your preaching and teaching but I'm tired of hearing about your 'gay lifestyle' all the time. You should just keep that private. No one wants to hear about it." The note was unsigned, and no return address was on the envelope. While I try to adhere to the common rule to ignore anonymous complaints, it still hurt. I can assure you that I do not share my "gay lifestyle" every week, whatever that means, and only in passing when I share a story that includes my wife Cindy or our son. But the note was clear: we like you but not all of you. That belief and privilege to even send that note came from somewhere. That theology of denying the core part of another one of G_d's creations and seeing me as fundamentally wrong is not gone in 2024. It is based in a culturally, theologically, and biblically formed understanding of my personhood, asserting that my whole being is not good enough to value. It is too often a request silencing the Queer voice in the room. It was a request to hide who I am. It says I am not enough. And it was a request to lie by omitting my "story" from the pulpit. Telling a "story" that does not anger others begins to be a habit in those environments. It's just safer.

It's not new in my life. My wife and I adopted a nine-month-old baby from Russia in 1999. We used an agency that had worked with gay couples often and they arranged for a required "home study" from a woman who was willing to write her report in a way that showed me as the mother adopting the child and that my partner (later my wife when we could legally get married in the US) as a "friend" who lived in the home with me. That "lie" was part of the entire process both here, and when we arrived in Russia to get our child. Cindy was always talked about as a friend who came to Russia with me. It was me who saw our adopted son first. We were told that he was very attached to the women who cared for him in the room where he was located and was quite shy. I walked toward him, and he literally flew into my arms, grabbed my shirt, and locked eyes with me. It was perfect and beautiful. Then he peed on me. Marking his mom. After they changed his clothes, I told them to hand him to my "friend." He smiled at her and laid his head on her shoulder. He was seeing his other mother in that sweet, sweet moment. He was ours. But all the agency paperwork and court documents both in the US and in Russia listed me as the sole mother. I stood in a Russian court and told them the lie. Inside I was thinking about Moses's mother, Jochebed. She was a mother who did what she had to do to keep her male baby safe during a time when the Egyptian rulers required all Hebrew male children to be executed so that the population of Jews did not continue to grow. Moses's mother set about with a plan to protect her boy and when the opportunity arose for her to serve as his "wet nurse," she hid her identity and nursed her son for twenty-four months. She lived the "lie" that protected her boy. Exodus 2:1–10 tells the story of that protective action.

> Now a man of the tribe of Levi married a Levite woman, and she became pregnant and gave birth to a son. When she saw that he was a fine child, she hid him for three months. But when she could hide him no longer, she got a papyrus basket for him and coated it with tar and pitch. Then she placed the child in it and put it among the reeds along the bank of the Nile. His sister stood at a distance to see what would happen to him.
>
> Then Pharaoh's daughter went down to the Nile to bathe, and her attendants were walking along the river-bank. She saw the basket among the reeds and sent her female slave to get it. She opened it and saw the baby. He was crying, and she felt sorry for him. "This is one of the Hebrew babies," she said.
>
> Then his sister asked Pharaoh's daughter, "Shall I go and get one of the Hebrew women to nurse the baby for you?"
>
> "Yes, go," she answered. So the girl went and got the baby's mother. Pharaoh's daughter said to her, "Take this baby and nurse him for me, and I will pay you." So the woman took the baby and nursed him. When the child grew older, she took him to Pharaoh's daughter and he became her son. She named him Moses, saying, "I drew him out of the water."[5]

5. Exodus 2:1–10, NRSV.

As I signed the final documents after the court hearing, there was no mention of Cindy, and there was no place for her to sign. It broke my heart, but it was necessary for that moment. Some asked why we didn't adopt a baby in the US, and we were quite honest about what we had been told in conversations with adoption agencies time and again: "A mother placing her child for an open adoption is not likely to choose a single woman" (me in the necessity to adopt in the US). Agencies in the US related to faith communities or founded by churches would not even talk to us. Their theology of G_d deeming Queer people as sinful and unacceptable was deeply embedded. The waiting period in nonreligious agencies was two to three years if we were to choose that route. Russia was the adoptive country of several of our lesbian friends' kids and my wife was a Russian history major in college. We did what we had to do. We lied. And after a nine-month adoptive process (yes, we saw the irony of the process taking nine months from start to finish), we brought our infant son home.

And in other spaces and places—in the church denomination and local church where I was serving—we continued the lie. Cindy was my dear friend who needed a place to live, and she would help with the baby. We now have an amazing twenty-five-year-old son who is wonderful, creative, messy, funny, and an all-American kid. He was told the adoption story from the earliest moments of his life, and he knows he has Russian blood running through his veins. His biggest regret is that his family history includes a receding hairline. His solution was to shave his head. He's ours. He has two moms. He is the proud kid of Queer parents. He has been taught to embrace a theology of acceptance, compassion, and inclusion. He understands G_d as more than any image or depiction he can imagine. We taught that to him, but first we taught him to love all persons no matter what. That's our core theology about G_d, that the divine loves us all. This theology is and always should be about loving others, no matter what.

Many Queer folx have hidden their sexuality—and it's not a preference like choosing an iPhone versus an Android phone or choosing chocolate versus vanilla ice cream—it is an inherent part of us but is not the only defining part of us. My friend Matt O'Rear often says that his sexuality is the least interesting thing about him. That's the truth. Being the authentic person you were born to be is vital for everyone, but it's imperative for Queer folx' very existence. Theologically we need to address why others make that one part of us the single thing that casts doubt on our worth and is used to deny us a place to be our divinely created selves. In the last chapters we have read about the historical, contextual, and biblical elements that are part of this story.

As I wrote the previous chapters about anti-Queer thinking and violence against the community, I reaffirmed my belief that theology is a root cause of the exclusion experienced by the Queer folx in faith communities of all kinds. The root cause is the historical, cultural, theological, and biblical understanding of those whose identities and sexuality is considered negatively. When I went to seminary at Saint Paul School of Theology in Kansas City, Missouri in the early 1990s, we had both out and closeted professors and administrators. We had several Queer students, although the students were out to each other but not to the wider SPST community due to our studies to enter ordained ministry in The United Methodist Church, which excludes out pastors. We were all on a journey to follow G_d's call on our lives despite that prohibition. The theology courses there were mostly based on love and acceptance of all, but I never heard that inclusion specifically including the Queer folx in the world. I never heard a fully inclusive understanding of G_d until I took a class with Dr. Emilie Townes and Dr. Tex Sample. They were bold and shared the BS of Queer hatred and oppression. Whoa! It was such a refreshing moment when they first addressed these issues. I was in awe. I was stunned. They were not perpetuating the theological "lie" that my very being was wrong on multiple levels. I cried as I sat there listening to them describe a theology based on full inclusion with an ethic of doing no harm to those we "othered." Tex even talked about the movement in the UMC to overturn the prohibitive language in the *Book of Discipline* against Queer clergy, doing gay weddings, or teaching about Queer lives. My eyes were opened, my heart began to be healed, my life was being honored and valued, and it was a total revelation. But still I hid.

Having a theology that was formed in the dusty towns of West Texas, being told that people like me were deviants and sinners, was harmful. My theology was formed by the fear I held onto with my family, hoping they never found out I was gay. My theology was formed in a well-hidden gay bar in Abilene, Texas seeing Queer bodies dance and love on one another, but making sure I looked both ways when I was entering or leaving the bar. My theology was formed by the last days of my gay friend dying of AIDS with no family having spoken to him in years. My theology was formed in that class taught by Tex and Emilie. My theology was formed by falling in love with my partner of thirty years and knowing G_d loves us—individually and together as a couple. My theology was formed one word at a time, one encounter at a time, and one moment of sharing the love of the divine at a time. The process took all of that and what I have heard during my sixty-some years of life. And my theology was formed by teaching our son what an inclusive and ever-expanding understanding of the divine's love for all creations challenges us to live into. We taught him that all folx in all shapes and sizes, in all genders and sexualities, in all races and creeds, and that in all places, at all times, for all people G_d's love always trumps any misreading of Scripture or cultural, negative expressions in the world. That is what I intend for preachers and leaders to learn and then share from this book. That is the reality I am trying to bring about in my own teaching and ministry. That is the truth about G_d's love for Queer folx everywhere, but I am also aware that the words in this book won't shake up the world. However, if these words and the preaching that comes from it changes one part of the world for a Queer kid sitting in their pews, then it's worth it.

The most helpful way of addressing a formed theology is to understand the stages of faith development from theologian James W. Fowler. He describes the ways we are formed in the faith from the earliest times in our lives to our full adulthood, in his book *Stages of Faith: The Psychology of Human Development and the*

Quest for Meaning. Fowler states that infants up to age two learn to trust through experiences with the world and the people who interact with them. When they experience loving comfort and an environment of care, they learn to trust the world that has been created for them by the divine and their families. When they are fed, hugged, changed, and protected they learn to depend on that behavior. It begins to form their worldview even from that early stage. Conversely, negative experiences like neglect and abuse will instill a lack of trust and a reality that does not include a sense of compassion or caring. This is an important part of forming "faith" in the world around them. Toddlers and young children aged three to seven are formed by story, image, and symbols that are shared from others and as a result G_d becomes an experiential part of their growth process. They are read and told stories about people, animals, and other story characters who share the acts of care and love each other. When we reach the ages of seven to twelve, we have developed a sense of right and wrong and an understanding of justice. This stage is likely when I learned and was formed to "see" G_d as an old white guy with questionable style choices. I heard judgment instead of justice and affirmation. The stage of twelve years to adulthood, "is characterized by the identification of the adolescent/adult with a religious institution, belief system, or authority, and the growth of a personal religious or spiritual identity. Conflicts that occur when one's beliefs are challenged are often ignored because they represent too much of a threat to one's faith-based identity."[6] Asking questions about what we have been taught and how our "theology" was formed is an important step in growth in the way we see the world. But it can still be quite complicated when someone is confronted by the teaching of the church and beginning to challenge those beliefs.

The next stage is seen in adults who are in their mid-twenties to their late thirties. A dawning of self and connections to the divine can bring a crisis of faith when their embedded beliefs and the teachings of the church or their ethical worldview begin to collide. This time can bring about a closer and more personal way

6. Armstrong, "Stages of Faith According to James W. Fowler."

of understanding and interpreting theological beliefs and assumptions. In later adulthood, some enter a final stage that is rarer than we might expect. "This stage is only rarely achieved by individuals. A person at this stage is not hemmed in by differences in religious or spiritual beliefs among people in the world but regards all beings as worthy of compassion and deep understanding. Here, individuals 'walk the talk' of the great religious traditions."[7] These stages of faith development have been evident for me as I reflect on my own faith development and my own experiences. Am I there yet? Is this my reality? Do I "walk the talk"? I think so, but I believe we all have moments of clarity and a consciousness that allows us to truly see everyone as worthy on every level. The opposite is also possible—the clarity that comes from older age can be contorted to move away from the teachings of the love of G_d and the life and teachings of Jesus. Media can cause us to dramatically shift our beliefs and distrust the "other." As mature adults we can still be changed to the negative—but also in more positive and affirming ways.

As I read again these stages of faith development from Fowler, I was reminded of the 1992 book by Craig O'Neill and Kathleen Ritter, *Coming Out Within: Stages of Spiritual Awakening for Lesbians and Gay Men.* One of the powerful images I took away from this book was that many Queer folx have experienced the church as a judgmental and unloving reality. "While some lesbians and gay men grow up with no religious bonding, many of those who do come to feel like abandoned children. When they look to their religions for an affirmation of their inherent goodness, a sense of community and belonging, and a viable pathway to a Creator, they often come away empty-handed."[8] I got the same empty-handed feeling when I was told Queer bodies were inherently bad, that Queer lives had to happen in secret, and that my future was one of isolation from friends and family due to the status of the church and culture around my very being. That feeling is hard to recover from. Living in fear is not what G_d ordained for any of their

7. Armstrong, "Stages of Faith According to James W. Fowler."
8. O'Neill and Ritter, *Coming Out From Within,* 35.

children—no matter their gender, gender expression, gender identity, sexuality, or any other way Queer folx define or choose not to define themselves. The "life image"[9] that we create and that is defined around us is hard to shift. Our family and faith craft significant and indelible imprints on us from our birth. Some are positive and some are negative. For the Queer community, sometimes the imprints of their birth family are impossible to change. In many instances, the creation of a "family of choice" is both necessary and life-giving. The ragtag, affirming, and diverse family chosen by circumstance or out of intentional planning, is the family that supports them and makes their vision of a family complete, especially when that Queer person has lost their birth family simply by coming out. Living a life "trying to become what they are not has a price."[10] And that price is steep.

> Asking people to repent for a condition of their very nature thrusts them into a powerful double bind: to engage in a constant struggle against core feelings of rightness and integrity or, on the other hand, to live as outcasts, feeling sinful. Crucial to a viable spiritual life image is a belief of being loved by a loving Creator. Feeling the way out of their double bind, many lesbians and gay people are left with a spiritual vision of disconnectedness and alienation from the Divine. As many gay men and lesbians imagine their future and do not see G_d [sic] walking with them.[11]

"Life image" is a phrase used by O'Neil and Ritter throughout their book. These "life images are models people have of how they expect their lives to proceed."[12] When culture, the church, and many families have a heteronormative life image of the proper way of being, Queer folx then don't fit as "normal" or as respectable participants in the world.[13] Queer folx need to hear something

---

9. O'Neill and Ritter, *Coming Out From Within*.

10. O'Neill and Ritter, *Coming Out From Within*, 5–6.

11. O'Neill and Ritter, *Coming Out From Within*, 35.

12. O'Neill and Ritter, *Coming Out From Within*, 5.

13. O'Neill and Ritter, *Coming Out From Within*.

powerful to counter all of that profound negativity. They need to hear a WORD that affirms them, honors their very being, and that helps to heal the wounds inflicted on them by the church, their families, and in their daily lives. That's exactly what I want for this book—to be a guide for preachers who are in those pulpits and places that caused the painful realities of heteronormative assumptions for so many of us. We need to feel loved and valued especially for who we are.

Patrick Cheng is very helpful regarding the theological assumptions and condemnation about Queer folx by others and the feeling that we just don't fit in. His book *Rainbow Theology: Bridging Race, Sexuality, and Spirit* is full of the experiences of a rainbow of scholars of color, but it also echoes the experiences of many Queer people, who are part of the rainbow.

> In some ways, the experience of LGBTIQ people of color can be characterized as never quite getting to Oz. That is, those of us who identify as queer are often stuck in the liminal space between Dorothy and Toto's monochromatic house from Kansas and the Technicolor hues of the Land of Oz. Although we may have been transported over the rainbow as a result of coming out of the closet, we are never able to walk out of the black and white doorway into a truly rainbow space—that is, a space in which the multicolored hues of our bodies, sexualities, and spiritualities are appreciated and seen as beautiful.[14]

What I hear and appreciate is the image of being caught in the middle. The reality of being unable to ever get to Oz resonated with me. There are spaces where I experience fear of rejection and I feel stuck and react both emotionally and physically. As a white woman I have unearned privilege that our siblings of color do not. Relating this image of being "stuck" is how many Queer folx in the church feel. They have heard so much condemnation from the church, which continues the centuries-old belief that persons with a same-sex loving orientation are condemned in the Bible. Additionally, they react to the things they have heard in the church,

14. Cheng, *Rainbow Theology*, xii.

but also from their family, in their homes and schools, from class-mates, from social media, and other negating persons and situations. They also receive these messages from their own imbedded theology of blessedness and acceptance by G_d, or the lack thereof. In essence, a theology of grace is vital to the Queer community if the monochromatic world they are living in can pierce the veil into a loving rainbow space. They need—we need—a space where the gorgeous hues of a rainbow space are a reality. That space does not come into being all by itself. If the church desires to be a rainbow-affirming space, preachers, pastors and congregants need to counter the historical, biblical, and theological underpinning of prejudice against the Queer community. This must be part of an intentional learning and growing process like the Reconciling in Christ process of the Evangelical Lutheran Church in America, the Dignity process in the Roman Catholic Church, and other movements in other denominational entities and processes.[15]

The job we have as preachers is holy and sacred. I was at a faculty party a few years ago that was on the Monday after Easter Sunday. The president of the seminary started his welcome and prayer saying he knew many of us were tired from "having" to preach on Easter Sunday. I immediately spoke out and said, "No, we *get* to preach Easter. And we get to do it every single time we gather as a community of Christian believers." It's an honor and a privilege to preach. Preachers must take seriously a new layer of interpretive and exegetical work in their preaching preparation, in addition to the work they already do. Countering a cultural and religious bias with our preaching and teaching can be tricky. I hear from students and other preachers that their churches do not want them to "be political" from the pulpit. Again, if I had a nickel for every time I have heard this from them and had it spoken into my own preaching experience, I'd be rich. Not private-plane rich

15. There are a number of denomination processes for recognizing a congregation who has intentionally done the work to proclaim their church as a reconciling partner. It is a recognition that some Queer folx look for before attending a particular church. Sometimes this is an official organization with the denomination and others are unofficial and provide a safe space to deal with the issues of both clergy and laity seeking resources.

but rich enough to travel more than I currently have the funds to accomplish. (Where should I go first?)

What our listeners in the pews mean by being "too political" is that they are being challenged to hear the Word reimagined from an inclusive and affirming perspective and that action forces them to examine their beliefs and worldviews. This shift will impact their understanding of marginalized Queer communities and potentially change their theology of G_d and the real design of a rainbow world. But those who complain are also confusing, in my opinion, political and partisan language. Partisan statements from the pulpit that attempt to guide voters or leaders to support a particular candidate or party is not okay. Jesus was as political as they come. He challenged the norms of society by welcoming those who were typically outcasts by eating with sinners, women of questionable backgrounds, and tax collectors, to name a few. He countered religious practices by healing on the Sabbath. He taught using language and imagery of the common people, including farming, fishing, and other vocations of the area where he found himself. Jesus entered Jerusalem on what Christians celebrate as Palm Sunday on a colt which had never before been ridden.

> After he had said this, he went on ahead, going up to Jerusalem. When he had come near Bethphage and Bethany, at the place called the Mount of Olives, he sent two of the disciples, saying, "Go into the village ahead of you, and as you enter it you will find tied there a colt that has never been ridden. Untie it and bring it here. If anyone asks you, 'Why are you untying it?' just say this, 'The Lord needs it.'"

> So those who were sent departed and found it as he had told them. As they were untying the colt, its owners asked them, "Why are you untying the colt?" They said, "The Lord needs it." Then they brought it to Jesus; and after throwing their cloaks on the colt, they set Jesus on it.

> As he rode along, people kept spreading their cloaks on the road. As he was now approaching the path down from the Mount of Olives, the whole multitude of the disciples began to praise God joyfully with a loud voice

for all the deeds of power that they had seen, saying, "Blessed is the king who comes in the name of the Lord! Peace in heaven, and glory in the highest heaven!" Some of the Pharisees in the crowd said to him, "Teacher, order your disciples to stop." He answered, "I tell you, if these were silent, the stones would shout out."[16]

The choice of the animal to ride into town was political. It was intentional. It was earth-shaking. During that time, no one rode an unridden colt into town except the king during a coronation procession. Jesus was countering that norm because he was not the "normal king" they knew from the present or the past. He was claiming the role prophesied from the Hebrew Bible. But he was also conspicuously saying, "Here I am. Come and get me. I'm not hiding from you or my destiny." The very act of entering the city in the way he did was political. What many parishioners hear as political is actually descriptions of how Jesus would chose to act and advocate if he were here in the present age.

How do we speak a new theologically relevant and affirming Word into the world when many are unprepared to hear that Word? As we learned from James W. Fowler in *Stages of Faith Development*, few adults make it to the stage of faith that is "walking the talk" through an acceptance of all persons and a willingness to be challenged about their earlier learnings and beliefs. My guess is that many adults in our pews are not there yet. Which opens the door to an invitation to study, to hear sermons, and to examine their long-held beliefs. An old preaching adage from Karl Barth states that preachers should preach with a Bible in one hand and a newspaper in the other.[17] Today preachers and their listeners have both and much more in the palm of their hand with a smartphone. You can't pretend that you don't know what's happening around the corner or around the globe. We live in an instantaneous information age. With twenty-four-hour news cycles touting their definition of "the truth," the church is badly needed to proclaim grace,

16. Luke 19:28–40, NRSV.

17. The origin of this phrase is attributed to Karl Barth but it's not entirely clear if he actually said it. See "Barth in Retirement."

forgiveness, and solidarity with those marginalized for being who and what they were/are created to be. My reading of Barth on the subject is that you interpret the news with the Bible. His intention was for preachers to read about the news of the world—whether it is devastating news about another senseless act of gun violence, a terrorist attack, the murder of a trans woman of color, the defacing and breaking of Jewish headstones, or an act of barbarism against gay men in Africa based on centuries of cultural indoctrination that is inherently heteronormative. The news is already traumatizing to the Queer community. It is trauma upon trauma piling on the heads and shoulders of people who are sensitive to these topics and have already lived through rejection, shame, judgment, and abandonment. Trauma-informed ministry sees that pain and seeks to heal the wounds of those folx. It is a style of ministry, teaching, preaching, and leading that is not only sensitive to the old and new wounds, but moves into a proactive and intentional ministry aware of the multi-trauma world in which the Queer community exists. It means creating a "Yes, Period" response to the Queer folx in your lives and in your pews as you preach, or as a layperson you lead a church council into an intentional process to being affirming and accepting in ways that result in concrete changes to you, your preaching, your people, and your ministry objectives and practices. Looking at the world in this way is more intentionally caring for those who still have open wounds.

Author Nadia Bolz-Weber often talks about preaching and leading from our scars and not our wounds.[18] Vulnerability is vital. To lead while our wound is still seeping blood means preaching from that place will be rooted in pain. When we preach and lead from our scars we have allowed ourselves to heal. We have done the work and taken the time for our wound to close—the scar may still be seen but the pain is hopefully somewhat gone and there are private wounds and scars no one ever sees. Imagine people in our pews whose wounds are not only still seeping blood, but they are infected and oozing pus. Imagine the many times folx sat in pews and heard preaching that inflicted new wounds to them or it

18. Bolz-Weber, "Preaching from Your Scars."

caused the opening of old ones. They sit there enduring deep cuts to their very being over and over through the churches' words or lack of words. All of this causes trauma and that is hard to move past. Next imagine the sermon they hear—either literally in church or in the world is a theology that continues to do harm. Queer folx have learned the places in the world where they can heal, where to avoid more harm, and where the danger of pain could be heaped pain upon pain. That's what this book is about. Creating trauma-informed and Queer-sensitive preaching can be the only place a Queer kid hears about their divinely given body and identity. Imagine a ten-year-old girl in church with her parents who feels to the very marrow of her bones that they are not Colleen, but Cody, and no one knows. Imagine hearing a heteronormative sermon about the sons and daughters of G_d with no awareness that that binary excludes them. And imagine two grandparents sitting in another pew whose grandson as come out to them in recent weeks. They are still processing the news and wondering if the things they were taught about "the gays" are true. Is their grandson going to hell? In their hearts and minds their precious grandson is still theirs. Will anyone reject them at church because of their Queer kid or grandkid? Then they hear a sermon from the pulpit of their church teach and preach that G_d's love is for all—straight, gay, lesbian, trans, old, young, rich, poor, short, tall, thin, heavy—and then imagine those binaries don't take center stage in those sermons and prayers. This is holy and important work.

Rainbow theology first arises out of the experience of Queer persons of color, but it is also more than that. It is about a "broader methodology and critique that can be applied to all forms of theological reflection."[19]

---

19. Cheng, *Rainbow Theology*, 85.

Chapter Five

Sexegetical Sermon Crafting

I AM USING THE words *sermon crafting* instead of the primary language that surrounds the act of "writing a sermon" in a very intentional way. When preachers "write" a sermon, they are usually writing a document that is geared toward reading—not geared toward speaking or hearing. Preachers must write for the ear.[1] This is a different way of creating the sermon. Listeners of sermons don't really want to hear about the Greek root of a biblical word to advocate for a particular point of view or interpretation. They don't want to hear the entire catalogue of conflicts and invasions of biblical lands. They also may not want to hear a deep dive into the political workings of a dysfunctional family from the Hebrew Bible. They want to hear a word from the Word. They want to hear about how their lives can be transformed by the love and grace of G_d. They want to hear the reality of doubt and about the lack of understanding by the disciples in the Gospel of Mark. They understand those kinds of internal and theological conflicts much more than they want to understand your knowledge of the nuances of Greek or Hebrew. I have made several biblical scholars very uncomfortable with this truth, but it is the truth, as I and many preachers have found in their own preaching experiences. People in your pews want to hear how they can better live out their faith

1. Wiseman, "Writing for the Ear."

in today's very complicated world. They want to know that they are not alone on this journey. They want relationships and community within a church body. And they want to know how to love others. I am basing this on multiple sources, including listening to listeners as John McClure points out in the book by that same name.[2] One of the interviewed persons for that book was Anthony. He said about his own preacher and his expectations of the sermon:

> Generally, it [preaching] touches your heart. It touches my heart when it touches my inner self, my inner feelings. The pastor that can do that to me, I feel that he [*sic*] can get to anybody. I consider myself a strong person but am also an emotional person to the degree of letting someone else say something which will touch me. You grow up. You're out there between streets and the church and activity outside of church that you have to grow up in. I just don't let everybody touch my feelings. It's very important to me when the pastor has the ability to do that. It's almost like the words that he [*sic*] says, he [*sic*] just touched your hand and [went] right through it.[3]

This act of "heart touching" is an important reminder to preachers that connections that have the capacity to touch the heart are so important and that preaching that connects to the listener's "inner feelings" in personal ways is impactful. Touching the inner person leaves a lasting lesson. The possibility of crafting a sermon that might spark a feeling of being seen and heard when preachers speak can be life-changing. We can extrapolate from there and from the pervasive anti-gay language in many churches and preached from many pulpits, that a sermon on the expansive love of G_d, a love that embraces Queer folx in ways that touch the heart and the inner self, can do the work of moving people to embrace a deeper inclusion in their hearts and in their churches. Think of that Queer kid sitting on the back row of the sanctuary, who is called names on their way home from school every single day and the pain they feel deep into their bones. Think of the power of the preacher to

2. McClure et al., *Listening to Listeners.*
3. McClure et al., *Listening to Listeners,* 23.

pierce the veil and say a word—a "heart-touching" word—that embraces and contradicts the very thing that young Queer person fears, the fear they will be found out and be rejected on every level—from their family and friends and from their school *and* church families. Preachers can counter that narrative when they emphatically and with authority state to that Queer kid that they actually belong and that they are a beloved child of G_d, no matter what. Think of the depth of despair of the mom on the seventh row whose husband just came out as bisexual and imagine her pain as she's searching for a way to love them despite the anxiousness she feels about anyone finding out their secret. Think of the act of declaring G_d's love for all. From those who want to tell this truth in a colloquialism that sounds Texan to me is "Y'all means ALL." Period. I wish I had found a way to feel that as a young Queer teen.

Their lives can change during your sermon. Their faith can change during your sermon. Words of affirmation and acceptance can transform those who are desperate for a word from the LORD stating that they are okay. I also ask you to think of the preacher who spews hatred and the damnation of our Queer siblings or of the "talking head" on one of the major news networks who blames, again, "the gays" for a hurricane hitting Florida. That language appears to be changing as culture shifts and as Queer lives are shown in a positive light in movies and television. That language also changes as more and more Queer folx live their lives more authentically and openly. There is still an unchallenged biblical and theological foundation that many of our churches and parts of our culture struggle with and that refuses to see the Queer community as it is being portrayed in positive ways in social and public media.

I remember the first Queer movie I ever saw. It was *Making Love,* starring Harry Hamlin, Michael Ontkean, and Kate Jackson. I had a crush on Kate Jackson from her *Charlie's Angels* days. I wanted to see her in the movie, and I wasn't really into the guys in the film, but she was enough. Additionally, the novelty of just seeing a gay movie was simply too much to pass up.

> *Making Love* was the first mainstream Hollywood drama
> to address the subjects of homosexuality, coming out

and the effect that being closeted and coming out has on a marriage. The film contrasts two visions of the "gay lifestyle." Zack wants to settle into a long-term monogamous relationship, while Bart is shown as promiscuous and uninterested in forming commitments.[4]

This story was about a married, seemingly straight man, played by Ontkean, coming to understand that he was gay. The openly gay character, Bart, played by Hamlin, was a sexually active gay man sleeping with multiple partners and doing drugs on occasion. This was not a positive image for this naive, young, Queer kid who had never had a real sexual encounter with anyone—let alone with a woman. I was still navigating coming out myself. But I also remember going to the latest show I could in February 1982 and hoping no one would recognize me in a ballcap and hoodie pulled up to hide my face. There were only a dozen others in the theater, and they too had on hats, scarves, or other items as "disguises." I wanted so desperately to see the movie and to have Queer lives validated. The story did not provide that for me, and I walked away with a hole in my heart. Evidently Kate was not enough for me, despite her sexy self and amazing hair. Instead, it reinforced the image of the hedonistic life of Queer persons, the isolation and sneaking around for love or what they could get that was close to that without committing to a real relationship, and the desperation to find a love that could last a lifetime with another person who fully "knew" you. I just wanted to see "me" on the screen. I wanted to see my life validated. What I did not get from *Making Love*, I got from Armistead Maupin's *More Tales from the City* in his "Letter to Mama."

> I'm sorry, Mama. Not for what I am, but for how you must feel at this moment. I know what that feeling is, for I felt it for most of my life. Revulsion, shame, disbelief —rejection through fear of something I knew, even as a child, was as basic to my nature as the color of my eyes.
>
> No, Mama, I wasn't "recruited." No seasoned homosexual ever served as my mentor. But you know what? I

4. Ryll, "Essential Gay Themed Films To Watch, Making Love."

wish someone had. I wish someone older than me and wiser than the people in Orlando had taken me aside and said, "You're all right, kid. You can grow up to be a doctor or a teacher just like anyone else. You're not crazy or sick or evil. You can succeed and be happy and find peace with friends—all kinds of friends—who don't give a damn who you go to bed with. Most of all, though, you can love and be loved, without hating yourself for it."

But no one ever said that to me, Mama. I had to find it out on my own, with the help of the city that has become my home. I know this may be hard for you to believe, but San Francisco is full of men and women, both straight and gay, who don't consider sexuality in measuring the worth of another human being.[5]

I cry every pride month when this piece pops up in my Facebook memories and I share it again for all to hear the truth that he was so fearful of how his mama would feel after reading those words. The fear is real. I lived that fear growing up and so have many Queer folx whose fear led them to live in the closet far too long and sadly, for many, this fear led them to deep depression, anxiety, and suicidal ideation, with many who completed their suicide attempts. The tragedy is painful to even think about or to read it in black and white.

The fear of stepping into a house of worship—church, cathedral, temple, mosque, home-based group, Bible study, or any other type of worshipping community—is real. Most Queer folx are afraid of how their parents and families will react to their revelation of being gay. They walk into a place of worship totally afraid at times. Some find a Queer-affirming church and are able to be present in all of their being. I celebrate that for those folx. Some search in their area for a community of faith that has a statement of faith that includes them. The congregation that I served for seven years, Gloria Dei Church in Huntingdon Valley, Pennsylvania, has a fabulous statement of faith they read every week as part of their worship.

---

5. Maulpin, *More Tales from the City,* 165–67.

We believe that the way we treat one another is the fullest expression of how we live out our faith. We find our approach to God through the life and teachings of Jesus Christ who is our model for living. We recognize the faithfulness of other paths which may also lead people to an experience of God. We stand in God's grace and we live that grace in our attitudes and actions toward one another. We understand the church as a community of people who together make up the body of Christ. We strive to serve the spiritual, emotional and physical needs of others. We are inclusive, as Christ was, and welcome all people seeking a closer relationship with God. We believe that the questions are as important as the answers, that living the mystery is a more sacred position than church tradition and doctrine. We strive to "love all, serve all, in Jesus' name" as we proclaim our mystery of faith that: Christ died . . . Christ has risen . . . Christ will come again.[6]

This statement is placed early in their worship service, and it is prominent on their web page. However, the church has struggled with the issue of homosexuality. A group tried to start the process to become a Reconciling in Christ congregation, a designation in the Evangelical Lutheran Church in America that shows a deep commitment to being inclusive and welcoming. That designation is a sign that the church has done the work to fully embrace the Queer community. The church tried a few years before I came to be their pastor. I asked what happened and they had no good answer other than they did it badly. No intention to try again any time soon. When I came on as a co-pastor my partner in ministry was an out, single gay man. He was a wonderful pastor and became a dear friend. That meant this church was being served by two out Queer folx. And they were not ready for starting the reconciling process. Seriously?

Within a few years my co-pastor was removed from the call by the congregational council for "pushing a gay agenda" when

---

6. Gloria Dei Church of Huntingdon Valley, PA. Statement of Faith, https://gloriadei.com/who-we-are/.

he preached. That left this out, married, Queer pastor to then be promoted to lead pastor. I, too, talked about my life and included my partner and son occasionally in some of those shared worship, teaching, and social moments. The tough thing was having Queer folx tell me they were excited to find our Statement of Faith online and came to worship with us. They wanted to feel a welcome without judgment about their tattoos, their clothing choices, and with their children who, just like other kids, made some noise during worship. Later I would follow up and hear a common theme. Our website indicated they would feel safe, but they shared "that only happened in your preaching and prayers." Others in the service and as they came and went "felt the church was judgy" and gave them a less that welcoming vibe. Some found our church more accepting and open than others. Clearly it didn't matter how much my preaching included, engaged, or connected dots for them— there was more needed. The intentional process to become reconciling was needed because that designation mattered. It provided a promise of some level of safety and hopefully bravery.

This is the reason I want us to do the work to create and craft sermons that are embedded in a process of teaching and intentional conversations that allows your church or ministry context to be ready to be a "worship home" for Queer folx, who despite the pain and judgment the church has caused, may be dipping their toes back into the water of a religious tradition for whatever reason. That is why this book has been such a personal and professional breakthrough for me, despite the pain it has caused to resurface.

I want to lead you into a profound and intentional way of embracing Queer folx into your community of faith and to preach that intentionality by using a method of sermon prep I call Sexegetical Sermon Crafting. It's a phrase I have coined intended to name and claim space for a brave new way of sermon crafting, which is rooted in inclusion and care. To begin this process, you must do some significant contextual analysis. Is your church already officially affirming through the denominational processes in place to create welcome? If so, how do you live that out? Do you and your church members understand that work? Do you have a table at the pride parade in your community or one nearby? Do your greeters understand and serve in a way to truly welcomes folx into your space regardless of their gender, gender expression, sexuality, marital status, and let's add mobility or handicapping conditions? If you don't know, you need to set up training opportunities for all who serve in that capacity in worship and on your church staff. This is the potential entry point for folks determining if your space is healthy and supportive of them and their families.

That leads to another profound question to address within your community. Do I begin this naming and claiming of safe space by dipping my toes into the water to list homophobia and transphobia in the prayers of the church? Do I list and affirm "all shapes and sizes of families" in my preaching and/or prayers? Or is there work to do first? Either way you can begin using a method of sermon crafting that will lead you, as the spiritual and pastoral presence in the church, to be more deeply embedded in the work that must be done to counter the historical, cultural, biblical, and theological assumptions that hinder welcome for the Queer community in many worshipping communities.

That first work of intentionality means observing your community setting and the need for conversations both inside and outside of the church community. Creating learning and listening events to process the "clobber texts" or explore the rich diversity of gender and gender expressions can be a start. Including preferred pronouns on your church nametags can set a tone of inclusion that presents itself from the moment a Queer family enters your space. But before that can happen, the work must be done so that your staff, leadership, and members understand the reason for these additions. That's part of the process of contextualization that is always the first step in Sexegetical preaching preparation. Whatever resources or processes the preacher employs, they should start with an embodied or sexual theology that makes sense and is open to allowing a discussion or preaching on the subject in an authentic and appropriate way. James Nelson, in *Body Theology*, says that this kind of sexual theology will understand our sexuality as intrinsic to the divine-human connection, as one of the great arenas for celebrating the Source of Life. Such theology will understand our sexuality as capable of expressing our intended destiny for freedom, creativity, vulnerability, joy and shalom. Such sexual theology will express the prophetic critique on every institutional and cultural arrangement that impacts our world.[7]

This kind of preaching begins from a place of justice and equality around issues of human sexuality. I believe we who would preach in this vein need a "sexegetical" theory for crafting sermons, preaching, and resourcing preaching on sexuality in the church.

In addition to the previous suggestions, preachers who are called to preach on the issue of human sexuality and gender are also encouraged to follow this sexegetical theory of homiletics by engaging in the questions and analysis outlined here:

- Do sexegesis on your congregation and/or community of faith.

  - Exegete your congregation by asking important questions, like who are they?

  - What is going on in their lives?

  - What is going on in the world around them?

  - What are the leading stories from the world and from their own communities?

  - What is their age, gender, gender expression, sexuality, race, socioeconomic, and cultural makeup?

  - What books are they reading, what music are they listening to, what are they watching on TV and/or seeing at the movies?

You learn these things through intentionally engaging in conversations within your community of faith—in social gatherings, during Bible study, and in other opportunities that arise in your ministry

7. Nelson, *Body Theology*, 22.

within your community. "Tea or Coffee with the Pastor" small groups helped me learn a lot about my congregation members. However, the development of deeper relationships brought on by seeing and hearing each other needs to be nurtured and brought into your conversations very intentionally.

These are important things to hear and observe and then to internalize for preaching in general and that can lead to a better understanding for the people in the pews listening to you. They want you to know them. They want to connect and hear stories and sermons that *speak to them and their context*. Telling a story about a West Coast person running to catch a ferry to get to work while you are in the rural Midwest church won't typically work. They likely have little to no personal experience with this reality. Maybe they saw Meredith and Derek riding a ferry on *Grey's Anatomy* over the years, but that is still not imbedded knowledge and experience. Telling a story about the rains impacting the harvest of beans in Kansas and wheat in Texas would probably work. I can tell a story about a horrible dust storm I encountered in Texas and the moment it also started raining. I was forced off the road to wait out the mud raining down from those two realities bumping into each other that day. I can express the fear I was having as a very new driver who was driving for the first time on a highway and not in town. There is a way to connect others to think about an experience they had that lead to fear. That works but I must speak to their heart to touch them. That "heart touching" from Anthony's interview shared earlier is so important. Getting in touch with the feelings of our listeners is paramount, however there are still going to be some for whom no "heart touching" is possible in their current understanding of Queer lives and faith. We still need to find those things that link their "beliefs" about the abomination of Queer folx to reconsidering that stance based on your intentional work to create an environment of welcome and then to understand there is another possibility of affirming G_d's precious Queer children. Their "No, Period" may be so deeply imbedded that they cannot move from their stance on these issues. And they may leave. That needs to be okay if true welcome is your goal.

Jesus knew his context and told stories appropriate to the location. "Heart touching" was his method of both teaching and preaching. He lived a life of affirmation and reaching out to the marginalized. And he knew his context. Jesus spoke about seeds and harvest in the crop lands, told stories about fishing and nets along the Jordan River and the Sea of Galilee, and he used the image of sheep and goats in the farmland where those animals were being raised. He paid attention to the context into which he spoke, taught, and preached. He knew where he was and what the listeners could relate to more fully. When you are determining how to address human sexuality and Queer issues, I want you to "do what Jesus would do," even if it is hard. Draw from the preponderance of texts where Jesus was reported as speaking words of inclusion, loving the marginalized, inviting sinners and "undesirables" to eat with him, and proclaiming the grace-filled kindom of G_d. That's what we preach using this first element of the Sexegetical Sermon Crafting Process.

Next we look at the important work of evaluating your context as it relates to human sexuality. To do this:

- Do sexegesis on your specific context related to human sexuality.
  - What is the makeup of the community of faith where you will preach this sermon?
  - Are there out Queer members in the community?
  - Will family members of Queer persons be present? Are you aware of them?
  - What experience does your congregation have around issues of discussing human sexuality?
  - Have you had adult or youth studies on the topic?
  - Is your context reconciling or open and affirming? If not, where do they stand on this process?

One of the harder elements to address in your community of faith is "knowing" whether or not there are Queer community connections in your pews. "Gaydar" is a hit-and-miss way of "knowing" who may or may not be part of the Queer community. It is flawed on so many levels. If a parent or teen hasn't come out to you and to others, how do you speak to that Queer kid being bullied every day and their parents who may be willing participants in the bullying of that kid? They also may not know a thing about what is happening in their kid's life. Delicately letting that kid know you are praying for them when you shake their hand as they leave church or doing a sermon series on the topic of faithful witnessing that addresses the pain in the world, including the pain of bullying, is a great start for that kid. Adding prayers for those who are not able to live fully into their authentic selves due to prejudice or ignorance can be a life vest thrown into the raging waters that kid is living in. If one time I was told in church that I belonged and that "telling people my truth" wouldn't result in ostracism I would have felt a three-thousand-pound weight lifted from my shoulders. My masseuse finds some of that weight whenever I go to her for a massage, but Maggie still tries to loosen the muscles of my still tightly wound body.

Telling someone my secret and being seen and heard didn't happen until that phone call with sharon, my mentor and dear friend, when I called her to tell her I was gay. Her response was a balm to the wound and lifted the weight I was carrying around with me all the time. It did not translate to my home, my community, or my school. I still kept the secret for my own safety and to keep the truce of not rocking the boat or to ensure that my parents still loved me. The secret was so powerful that I was sinking under the weight of it. Often, I am so tuned to that memory that I can spot it in another person. Still, it's not enough to say "Me, too." There has to be an intentional process of gaining trust by discussing these issues and dismantling the "clobber texts" that have led to prejudice and exclusion. That's what I feared and is also what many Queer folx fear in their life journey. This is especially true if the larger church and the faith communities they have been part of are perpetuating the exclusive beliefs of the church of their youth or is the one faith community that has cast them out.

Next you need to not only know the stance of your congregation and any governing bodies associated with it, but you also need to explore the ways that stance is impacting those in the world beyond decisions of polity in your larger church. So,

- Do sexegesis on your denominational polity and doctrine.
  - What does your denomination teach about human sexuality?
  - What is their position on gender, gender expression, or nonbinary identity?
  - If your denominational polity and/or doctrine on the issues of human sexuality and gender is different than your own or your church's, how will you address this issue?
  - What about persons in your congregation who have a different perspective than yours or the denomination's?
  - How will you navigate this difference of perspective and for what purpose are you doing this preaching?
  - Who might be the initial conversation partners? Your church leadership? Others?

Growing up in the Northwest Texas Annual Conference of the United Methodist Church, I didn't know that the international church body that determines the polity and doctrine of the church had deemed me "incompatible to Christian teaching" for some time after it was adjudicated. But now I hear it again and again as the global Wesleyan church wrestles with the stance on Queer folx. Learning who I was inevitably led to a stalemate between who I believed G_d was calling me to be and a church that considered me an abomination. These two worlds crashed at that youth gathering where we talked about the 1972 decision. I have watched denomination after denomination deal badly with issues of sexuality and gender. I have watched friends and colleagues pushed out of their churches both as laity and as clergy. When a confirmation group in Omaha, Nebraska refused to join the church because of the polity of the church around Queer issues,[8] my heart broke, but it also saw hope in the future of addressing sexuality and gender. There has been a split of my former church more recently. A Global Methodist Church has formed and both churches and clergy have left the UMC to be part of that global church, primarily because they continue to push an anti-gay agenda and to perpetuate the "incompatibility" language about Queer folx. There have been a significant number of friends and former students who have chosen to disaffiliate from the UMC and that knowledge has been depressing at times. In Amarillo, Texas, a community I lived in during my youth and as a junior high school social studies teacher, every single United Methodist Church chose to disaffiliate and go to the GMC. That news was stunning to me. There was not one UMC to serve members who did not agree with the disaffiliation. Two women I know have planted a new church there and are meeting with over 150 people in worship since they opened their doors in early June of 2023.

When an entire city's UM churches choose to embrace the anti-Queer teachings of a global denomination, it can feel like the world is collapsing to a Queer kid losing their pastor and church. It can feel isolating and demoralizing to a woman whose husband has just come out to her as gay. These folx have been abandoned by their church. That leaves a lasting legacy. I've been there, done that, and chosen not to buy the T-shirt. When my district superintendent said relinquish your ordination or face charges when we announced our wedding, all that fear of the church finding out turned so dang quickly to abject anger and then to a peace that leaving the UMC was the best thing for me to do. The relief that came—with personal reflection and processing with my therapist—told me it was the right decision. An entire denomination had turned its back on the Queer community in 1972. It had walked away. It had embraced a "No, period" about Queer lives being beloved or even divinely created. It's been fought over since then in small Sunday schools rooms, church council meetings,

8. "Omaha confirmation class chooses to delay becoming members of United Methodist Church."

Annual Conference sessions, and during the quadrennial General Conference sessions. The fact I held out so long is astonishing to me now. Why didn't I leave sooner? I'm not sure. But I know this truth: when the church goes after you, you have to get out and help others get them out too.

So, as you navigate the polity of your own congregations and denominations as a whole, I believe that the next step in the Sexegetical Process is to ask why you might be choosing to preach a specific sermon on human sexuality and gender and how you are crafting that sermon. Why now? Why here?

- Do sexegesis on the situation and support for preaching on the topic.

  - Who is your target audience?

  - Do you have "buy-in" from your church and/or church leadership for preaching on this subject?

  - How are you preparing your community to receive this word?

  - Is there a situation brewing that is leading to this (baptism of gay couple's child, recent sexual assault, human sexuality study going on with adults or youth, etc.)?

  - How will you prepare the folks most closely related to this situation to hear this sermon?[9]

I love the poem "A Prayer for My Queer and Trans Siblings." Someone at a conference shared it with me. I have not been preaching recently but I keep thinking that this poem needs to be spoken from the pulpit, by me or another pastor, in a church out there trying to do the work of creating full inclusion and affirmation of our Queer siblings. What if that Queer or trans kid heard this from the pulpit? What if this was a reading for the day? What if this was shared in a church email or web page? Would it have changed my life and shaped my "secret" beyond the hurt and pain I

---

9. Wiseman, "'Sexegetical' Theory for Preparing to Preach on Human Sexuality."

experienced as a high school kid in West Texas? First, that it would even be spoken in a place of worship or by a clergy person would have blown my mind. Second, that while not explicitly saying the words *Queer* and *Trans Siblings* except in the title, I hear a Word from the Lord in this prayer that affirms my body, my sexuality, and all of who I am. Think about that Queer or questioning youth contemplating suicide and what might happen in the reading and hearing of this poem. I leave it here to end this chapter because it speaks louder than I can.

A Prayer for My Queer and Trans Siblings

"Here you are.
Here, in this holy space,
on this ground that is holy
because you are here.

Here you are, in flesh and bone,
filling up this body that belongs to you alone.
Your pumping heart is a wonder
because it keeps you alive.
Your loving heart is a blessing
because it keeps all of us alive.

The Spirit of Love has a home in you.
May we all see that love in you
and let our hearts become mirrors
for the compassion at your core.

The Spirit of Justice has a home in you.
May we light our wicks
from one another until we are all aflame,
until we burn out every prejudice
we carry in these bones.

Here you are.
Holy as you are.

Blessed be.[10]

---

10. Reynolds, *Love Like Thunder.*

Chapter Six

Queering the Pulpit

A Case Study

FROM THE OUTSET OF this book's initial formation and throughout it's writing, I have dreamed of one Queer kid, one local drag queen, or one nonbinary couple to hear an affirming word from the Lord from the pulpits of churches far and wide. Maybe that's too high of a goal. Maybe it's more about that one kid, that one drag queen, and that one couple finding safer and *braver* space to be who they are. But also, to be in the midst of a group of believers and their leaders who are intentionally working to share the message that those Queer folx are precious and adored by the G_d who created them to be themselves. I want preachers and communities of faith to begin the process of reexamining broadly and locally their history, their cultural circumstances, their understanding of Scripture, and their theology for those couple of persons who may still be sitting in their pews. Or their parents and grandparents. Or the lesbian who wears her complete cowboy outfit to church jingling her spurs on the linoleum floor, walking proudly up the center aisle of the church. Because everything starts locally. Change typically doesn't happen overnight and it does not begin with a reach that is far and wide. It takes one pastor, one church, one church leadership team, and one congregation to bring about change and transformation, welcome, and affirmation. Maybe that's really what I want. Because

I firmly believe that is what G_d wants, too. I believe to the core of my being that a real transformation can happen when we address these issues and allow the abundance of G_d's love and grace to be shared more boldly and maybe even flamboyantly for everyone. Remember, "Y'all means ALL."

Unfortunately, many preachers don't believe in the specificity of justice preaching in general, let alone about Queer lives. We can, they can, we all can find a way forward that brings about justice and proclaims a specific love for all—more than that especially to the Queer community. To do this I lean heavily on Christine Smith's work in *Preaching Justice: Ethnic and Cultural Perspectives*. In it she challenges preachers to move beyond universal grace. For me and my Queer siblings, we don't just want to hear "G_d loves all of you and forgives each and every one of you" in preaching. We want to specifically hear that G_d loves that Queer kid being bullied on the way to and from school every single day. And I want to hear a covenant with that kid, Paul with his pink hair, bow tie, and perfectly selected outfit, that announces he needs be known and cherished in his home and community. If the words aren't spoken then and there, I want that kid to find acceptance and safety in a community of faith. That does not happen overnight. It takes time. But you start that journey by moving away from "generalization, universal claims, and assumed truths put forth from voices of power and privilege."[1] We need to understand the role of preachers who are not only invited but are called to enter pulpits and platforms to preach the Word of G_d's abundant love. We cannot do that without "claim[ing] the truth that all preaching is done within very particular social and religious communities, and it is thoroughly influenced by the social location of a particular preacher."[2] Maybe the best thing to remember is that you may be the one person with the possibility of standing between that pink-haired kid and the kids who are bullying him, because all of them are members of your church. Maybe the change must start with you. Reading this book is a start to hearing a redefining of truth, to

1. Smith, ed., *Preaching Justice*, 134.
2. Smith, ed., *Preaching Justice*, 134.

stretch your assumptions and previous teaching and learning, and to find a new way of being an ally not just from the pulpit but also in the community in which you live and work.

One thing that is important to understand is that not all Queer folx are interested in coming into a church building like the one they left or the one that left them. Just as all people, groups, and contexts are not the same, the wishes of the Queer community to engage in religious communities are as varied as the words that try, and too often fail, to describe them. Smith believes there are three primary groups within the Queer community and those led to preaching that might be done in the church to varying effectiveness. We need to consider them intentionally. One group of Queer folx "want to be integrated into mainstream culture and the church with all of the rights, privileges, and acknowledgments that accompany heterosexual relationships."[3] Preaching that addresses this perspective means highlighting equality for all. It would strongly echo the need for equality with others in their work, faith, and cultural settings. However, this type of preaching does not speak to the specificity of Queer lives and their needs. It does not address the trauma Queer lives have experienced in the church and in the world. The gap between what is said and what is really meant by the word of grace proclaimed generally for all people needs to do more to begin to heal the wounds Queer folx carry. Sure, universality is good, but it does not dig deeply into the core of much needed affirmation, apologies, and advocacy in this work.[4]

Another group of Queer people are working to create a movement to change the way the Queer community is seen by others. This group wants to move away from simply saying "we are all loved and given grace" to a specific calling out of anti-Queer behavior in the church and beyond. Those in this group want to speak into the specific desire to live more authentically and with a freedom of expressing their lives openly. Preaching from this perspective means we preach and minister in ways that highlight a "sacramental understanding of human embodiment, sexuality,

3. Smith, ed., *Preaching Justice*, 136.
4. Smith, ed., *Preaching Justice*, 136–37.

and relationality, and the justice of all people's sexual and relational expressions being acknowledged, respected, and treated as incarnational goodness."[5] We move from everyone belonging and being loved—at least in the spoken word in the first type—to everyone's embodied self being specifically celebrated as sacred. However, there is still no clear wresting with the systemic issues involved in the way the church and the world have traumatized, stigmatized, and marginalized the Queer community. It stops short of declaring Queer bodies being created by and celebrated by the divine. There is still no addressing of the specificity of Queer bodies being violated or being attacked. This type of preaching is not yet ready to move folks from their pew seats into the world to advocate for Queer folx and it does nothing much to change anything in the world.[6]

The third group is advocating for a brand-new way of seeing life in general and advocating for Queer lives specifically to be seen and affirmed. It longs to "shape a new understanding of relational life, gender identity (gender fullness or gender independence, rather than gender complementarity), sexuality, community, covenant relationships, theology, and spirituality."[7] Preaching from this need leads the preacher and the people in the pews to critique previous understandings of human sexuality and gender identity. This critique leads folx to radically call out homophobia and transphobia and it leads to the active and engaging work of justice and equality. Preaching from this perspective also understands that merely tolerating or marginally affirming the Queer community will never be enough. Critiques and deconstructing of previous beliefs and practices must be done. According to Smith, this is when preachers "might name and indict the many and varied oppressive forces of heterosexist privilege and domination and proclaim the vision of a world free from restrictive and violating gender constraints and idolatrous sexualities."[8]

5. Smith, ed., *Preaching Justice,* 137.
6. Smith, ed., *Preaching Justice,* 137.
7. Smith, ed., *Preaching Justice,* 137.
8. Smith, ed., *Preaching Justice,* 137.

For me this plays out in several ways. Let's assume these perspectives are echoed in Queer folx, the pastor, and the congregation where you are serving as a pastor. I ask what did you say from the pulpit when twenty-six people—twenty of them second graders—were killed in their classroom inside the Sandy Hook Elementary School in Newtown, Connecticut in 2012? Did you simply say "we pray for everyone who suffers in our world?" Or did you say "we pray for those whose lives have tragically been taken through the epidemic of gun violence in our country"? Or did you specifically name the twenty-six people, all precious, beloved ones of the kindom of G_d, in Sandy Hook, and declare that we are called by our covenant of care about and help end this madness? On that morning many preachers changed their sermons and added to their written prayers. Others had vigils or prayer circles come together in their shock and grief. They acknowledged the shared grief of our nation upon hearing this latest act of horrific gun violence. Many churches handed out prayer cards to send to Sandy Hook. Some invited members to call their state and national representatives to talk about the need for sensible gun reform, some even placing call lists of local and national leaders on a table at the entry points in their buildings in hopes that they would call to help in active advocacy.

To push this further, I ask another question for preachers. When the Pulse nightclub shooting happened on Latin night in Orlando, Florida, in 2017, what did you pray about? Did you acknowledge that Pulse is a gay nightclub and that the vast majority of those present were Latinx? Did you even mention it? At your church was it in the prayers? Did the preacher change what they were preaching about that next morning? Were the names called out? Did it get any attention in your religious community? There were forty-nine killed and fifty-three injured by a homophobic and violent young man who entered the club and starting shooting. It is the deadliest incident of violence against LGBT [*sic*] people in the United States, surpassing the UpStairs Lounge arson attack in 1973.[9] For Queer folx who were still sitting in pews or listening in

9. "Pulse Nightclub Shooting."

to their families or friends talking about the services they attended, many heard nothing. Not one word was spoken about Pulse. Not one word about the two hundred-plus rounds that were shot into that club or the hostage situation that ensued with a number of those present trapped in a bathroom with the shooter. Preaching that is too general and way too often out of touch with the concerns and pain of our Queer siblings has continued to erode an already fragile relationship with them and the church. Being more connected to the context, doing the sexegetical work to craft new ways of preaching justice for all—but also specifically for Queer folx—needs to happen from the inside out. And the community needs to hear those words spoken out loud and clearly articulated from the pulpits of our churches. Bold, brave, and beautiful words of care and compassion for the Queer community need to be proclaimed. The gospel of Jesus Christ calls us to lead and to lean into the potential role we can play even if it's just for Paul and for that one drag queen and that one non-binary couple hoping someone cares enough to "preach the damn gospel"[10] on that day, in their church, and into the hearts and minds of those present.

How do we start? Gently and personally, we need to tackle these hard things with the intentionality of the holy work that it is. After doing the work on yourself and with your community of faith the next step is making connections to the Queer community—one person at a time or maybe doing something completely and an amazingly Queer-drenched holy combination. So again, how do we start? We apologize to those who have been hurt by the church over and over and over again and we make that apology the begging of our work for Queered pulpit and pews. We also pray for all the ways the church has failed to love and honor who G_d made them to be. We have to plainly and specifically state the harm inflicted by the church and its members. The distrust, pain, and trauma that many in the Queer community feel must

---

10. This phrase was first spoken to me by a colleague, Dr. Timothy J. Wengert, at United Lutheran Seminary in Philadelphia. It was so popular with our students that they made T-shirts with the phrase on it. I echo that call often in my own teaching.

be addressed and mitigated if a connection and invitation to even enter the church is desired or possible. Doing the sexegetical work of discerning your community is imperative.

As an example of what might be next, I share the story of "Drag Me to Church," an event done in collaboration between the Atlanta Pride Committee and the St. Luke Lutheran Church in Atlanta, Georgia, a fully reconciling and welcoming congregation of the ELCA. They had formed relationships during Pride events and within the community where the church is located. The pastor, the congregation, the bishop of the synod, and the church leadership team did the hard work to connect with the Queer community for an amazing event from the beginning. From the church's press release:

> St. Luke Lutheran Church, Atlanta, Georgia, an inclusive and affirming congregation of the Evangelical Lutheran Church in America (ELCA), proudly announces a special worship service in partnership with The Atlanta Pride Committee to commemorate the historic Stonewall Riots. "Drag Me To Church," to be held on June 25, 2023, at six o'clock PM, will feature the participation of talented Atlanta-based drag queens, serving as a testament to our church's commitment to continuing the work of Jesus by standing with the oppressed community and those on the margins.[11]

Pastor Matt O'Rear, an out gay pastor, knew this event was fraught with the possibility of going badly if they did not use caution, careful planning, and intentional collaboration, but he also knew that it was deeply needed to extend a hand of love and grace specifically to the needs of Queer folx. The drag community had every reason to be suspicious if a church out of the blue invited them to come "perform" at a church event, but that's not what Pastor Matt and the Pride Committee wanted to provide. They had a clear purpose and an answer to the Why? question.

> The idea for Drag Me to Church came about as a collaborative effort between St. Luke Lutheran Church,

11. Press release shared by Rev. Matt O'Rear on August 15, 2023.

the Atlanta Pride Committee, and our deep reverence for the historic Stonewall riots. We wanted to create an event that honors the legacy of Stonewall while celebrating the vibrant artistry of drag within the inclusive and welcoming embrace of our church community. It is a commemoration of love, diversity, and unity, where we come together to honor the courageous acts of resistance that sparked a movement for LGBTQ+ rights.

It is crucial for St. Luke Lutheran to show up, show out, and support the Atlanta LGBTQ+ community, especially in light of our current political atmosphere. We are deeply aware of the ongoing challenges and threats faced by the LGBTQ+ community. We firmly believe in the inherent worth and dignity of every individual, and it is our mission to be a steadfast source of love, acceptance, and inclusivity. By hosting Drag Me to Church, we aim to create a sacred and transformative space where LGBTQ+ individuals can freely express their identities and spirituality. This event is our way of honoring the courageous acts of resistance at Stonewall and providing a welcoming environment that celebrates the beauty and strength of the LGBTQ+ community.[12]

The perceived need for this kind of service came out of the conversations—holy conversations—about the pain many Queer folx have felt at the hands of churches large and small. The specific pain and threats to the Queer community were acknowledged from the beginning planning of this event. There was a clear commitment to being a place of healing and grace for a specific community through this worship service.

That night this little Lutheran church that averaged thirty-five people in worship on Sundays opened their doors to over two hundred people, some members of the church but also many who weren't. Some were part of the alphabet soup that tries to define our community. Many were Queer folx in the ever-expanding understanding of their multiplicity of identities. The pastor wore a clergy shirt and robe, some wore their drag queen attire with

12. Materials prepared for the church and The Atlanta Pride Committee shared by Rev. Matt O'Rear, August 15, 2023.

their identities on full display, and others just showed up in what defines their gender or Queer identity. When the electricity went out just before the service, they found and lit Advent candles left over from December. When the prayers were read and the songs were sung by a number of drag performers you could see a light appearing in the darkness that was not just the flickering candles in that holy space that holy night. The spark of that service was about transforming the relationship between the Queer community in Atlanta and a little church that could and did want to enter into that holy work.

The sermon, preached by Pastor Matt, was one of the most loving and prayerful sermons I have heard as a Queer person. It was specific about the pain and loss for many in the Queer community of a church that moved away from them and has not returned from the far country. I include it with his permission.

> *Usually, I stand before this congregation every Sunday with what I think is a clear message, ready to share the teachings of our faith. Albeit, it's a short sermon most Sundays. Tonight's will be even shorter. Yet, as I thought about this reflection on this special worship, words seemed to elude me. Instead, the phrase that reverberated was: "What is a pastor to say?"*
>
> *What is a pastor to say in moments like these?*
> *What is a pastor to say on a night like this?*
>
> *What is a pastor to say when the air is filled with love, overflowing from every corner of the church? And I mean every corner!*
>
> *What is a pastor to say when the script of our welcome statement, written in the sacred words of Romans 15:7, "Welcome one another, therefore, as Christ has welcomed you," comes alive before our very eyes? A welcome that has echoed through the halls of our congregation for more than thirty years.*
>
> *What is a pastor to say when the resilient souls of St. Luke Lutheran have worked tirelessly to create a sanctuary, a brave space where all are embraced?*

What is a pastor to say when our humble little Lutheran church has joined hands with one of the pioneering pride committees in the world, standing side by side with the At-lanta Pride Committee, to make this night a reality?

What is a pastor to say when this assembly rises in unison, paying tribute to those who paved the way, bravely fight-ing for our rights at the hallowed grounds of the Stonewall Inn?

What is a pastor to say when the vibrant artistry of drag unfurls like a sacred tapestry, weaving together the diverse threads of God's creation?

What is a pastor to say when this pastor knows that there is no modern-day drag culture or LGBTQ+ civil rights movement without the bravery of trans women, especially BIPOC trans women, who paved the way?

In all these moments, dear friends, this pastor can only say a few sacred words, "It's about damn time!" Thanks be to God!

It's about damn time that we embrace our shared human-ity and recognize that love knows no bounds. Can I get an amen? It is a time to honor the beauty of the diversity of all of God's children, to stand tall and proud in the knowledge that we are fearfully and wonderfully made.

So let us lift our voices in joyous harmony, celebrating the richness of our identities and the unconditional love that surrounds us. Let us march forward hand in hand from this sanctuary, guided by the teaching of Jesus of compas-sion, acceptance, and justice.

In these moments, let the Holy Spirit move where she wills, igniting the flame of hope and renewing by the power of unity. Together, let us create a world where every individu-al, regardless of who they love or how they identify, or how they express themselves, is fully embraced and celebrated as God's beloved.

Dear friends, I stand here humbled and grateful for this gathering of love, acceptance, and profound grace. May the joy of this moment reverberate within our hearts, and may the spirit of this night that fills this sanctuary inspire us to push forth back into the world with the message of radical love because that's God's love.

May the love of God continue to guide us, uplift us, and transform us into beacons of light in a world that is desperately hurting. Friends, let us be grace in action to this world. Amen.

This sermon was the perfect one for that moment, in that place, for those people. It spoke volumes about the role that preaching, worship, advocacy, and collaboration can make in a little church in the South. It specifically spoke to the marginalization and ostracism that has too often been the relationship between the church and the Queer community. And it spoke to the heart of the gospel—that G_d's love is for all—but specifically that night and into the future it was about the drag performers, their partners and friends, Queer members of the congregation, and the Queer and straight members in that community. What I would have given to have anything like this to open the church back up for me. What I would have given to find a place that publicly shines the light on the sacredness of my Queer body. What I would have given to hear a Word from the Lord, sung in candlelight by a church committed to be a transformational place to let the Queer and Queer-affirming folx' light shine.

From the beginning of this book, I have worried that it is too personal, that my story didn't need to be so imbedded in the stories and the ways I challenge the historical development, cultural pressures and experiences, interpretative biblical tradition and assumptions, and the theological processes that have led us to a place of condemnation and ostracism of our Queer siblings. I wanted to invite you to that holy and hard work. I know it's hard. As I wondered about my story being present, I listened to my friend Matt talk about the heart-touching moment that happened from reimagining the connection between the church and the Queer community. I listened to my friend Brian in that hospital bed asking, pleading with me to touch him—to really touch him. I listened to that little girl jingling her spurs up the church aisle and to her fear while hiding who she was for so long. I listened to Paul with the pink hair and the bow tie tell me he was being bullied. And I listened to Susan whispering into my ear that she is gay and is proudly asking her girlfriend to go to the prom with her. I listened to sharon tell me on the fearful phone call that she knew and she loved me fully just as I am. And I listened to the still, small voice in the wilderness praying for a place to hear that G_d specifically, intentionally, and unashamedly loves all of who they are. Wouldn't that be worth the work that needs to be done in our churches and in our world? Wouldn't that be worth challenging our preconceived notions of who belongs and who does not? Wouldn't it be worth saving one more Queer teen contemplating suicide because they have never heard that G_d loves them—not in spite of who they are and who they love—but because they were created just as they are?

Wouldn't that be worth it?

"Yes, PERIOD!"

That's what G_d says, "Yes, PERIOD!"

And that is the work you are called to do.

Say it again, "Yes, PERIOD!"

Bibliography

Armstrong, Thomas. "The Stages of Faith According to James W. Fowler." American Institute for Learning and Human Development, June 12, 2020. https://www.institute4learning.com/2020/06/12/the-stages-of-faith-according-to-james-w-fowler/.

Associated Press. "California shop owner killed over Pride flag was adamant she would never take it down." https://www.politico.com/news/2023/08/23/california-pride-flag-killing-carleton-00112570.

"Barth in Retirement." *Time*, May 31, 1963. https://content.time.com/time/subscriber/article/0,33009,896838,00.html.

Berlin, Adele, and Marc Zvi Brettler. *The Jewish Study Bible*. New York: Oxford University Press, 2004.

Bolz-Weber, Nadia. "Preaching from Your Scars." The Corners, April 9, 2023. https://thecorners.substack.com/p/resurrection-is-messy.

The Book of Discipline of the United Methodist Church, 2012. Nashville: United Methodist Publishing House, 2016.

Boswell, John. "The Church and the Homosexual: An Historical Perspective." Keynote address to the Fourth Biennial International Convention at Fordham University, 1979. http://www.fordham.edu/halsall/pwh/1979boswell.html.

Carlo, Andrea. "Why It Took Decades for LGBTQ Stories to Be Included in Holocaust History. *Time*, April 7, 2021.

Cheng, Patrick S. *Rainbow Theology: Bridging Race, Sexuality, and Spirit*. New York: Seabury, 2013.

Downs, James. *Stand By Me: The Forgotten History of Gay Liberation*. Athens, GA: University of Georgia Press, 2020.

Duberman, Martin Bauml, Martha Vicinus, and George Chauncey Jr. *Hidden from History: Reclaiming the Gay and Lesbian Past*. New York: New American Library, 1989.

Durgen, Celina, and Dru Johnson, eds. *The Biblical World of Gender: The Daily Lives of Ancient Women and Men*. Eugene, OR: Cascade, 2022.

Faughndur, Ryan. "Inside the right's 'moral war against Disney' as Florida Culture Conflict Intensifies." *Los Angeles Times*, April 15, 2022. https://

Bibliography

www.latimes.com/entertainment-arts/business/story/2022–04–15/in-disney-desantis-feud-echoes-of-a-long-culture-war-with-the-religious-right.

Finke, Leigh. *Queerfully and Wonderfully Made: A Guide for LGBTQ+ Christian Teens*. Minneapolis: Beaming, 2020.

"Gay Men Under the Nazi Regime." *The Holocaust Encyclopedia* from the United States Holocaust Memorial Museum. https://encyclopedia.ushmm.org/content/en/article/gay-men-under-the-nazi-regime.

Gilad, Elon. "Judaism and Homosexuality: A Brief History." June 6, 2016. https://www.haaretz.com/jewish/2016-06-02/ty-article-magazine/.premium/judaism-and-homosexuality-a-brief-history/0000017f-e6a5-dc7e-adff-f6adec1f0000.

Kuhn, Karl A. "Natural and Unnatural Relations Between Text and Context." *Currents in Theology and Mission* 33 (2006) 313–17.

Martin, Colby. *Unclobber: Rethinking our Misuse of the Bible on Homosexuality*. Louisville: Westminster John Knox, 2016.

Maulpin, Armistead. *More Tales from the City*. New York: Harper Perennial, 1980.

McClure, John, Ronald J. Allen, Dale P. Andrews, L. Susan Bond, Dan P. Mosely, and G. Lee Ramsey Jr. *Listening to Listeners: Homiletical Case Studies*. Saint Louis: Chalice, 2004.

Mechelke, J. D. "The Call to Queerness." *Church Anew*, June 16, 2022. https://churchanew.org/blog/posts/jd-mechelke-the-call-to-queerness-h5se6?mc_cid=9b8a8380ee&mc_eid=2e8fadd76e.

Murphy, David J. "More Evidence Pertaining to 'Their Females' in Romans 1:26." *JBL* 138 (2019) 221–22.

Nelson, James B. *Body Theology*. Louisville: Westminster John Knox, 1992.

"Omaha confirmation class chooses to delay becoming members of United Methodist Church." *Great Plains News*, April 30, 2019. https://www.greatplainsumc.org/newsdetail/omaha-confirmation-class-refuses-to-become-members-of-united-methodist-church-12803676.

O'Neill, Craig, and Kathleen Ritter. *Coming Out From Within: Stages of Spiritual Awakening for Lesbians and Gay Men*. San Francisco: HarperSanFrancisco, 1992.

Outler, Albert C., ed. *John Wesley*. Oxford: Oxford University Press, 1964.

"Pulse Nightclub Shooting." *Wikipedia*. https://en.wikipedia.org/wiki/Orlando_nightclub_shooting#Perpetrator.

Reynolds, Jess. *Love Like Thunder*. https://skinnerhousebooks.tumblr.com/post/653876946900500480/a-prayer-for-my-queer-and-trans-siblings-here-you.

Richards, E. Randolph, and Brandon J. O'Brien. *Misreading Scripture with Western Eyes: Removing Cultural Blinders to Better Understanding the Bible*. Downers Grove, IL: InterVarsity, 2012.

Bibliography

Riggle, Ellen D., and Sharon Rostosky. *A Positive View of LGBTQ: Embracing Identity and Cultivating Well Being.* Lanham, MD: Rowman and Littlefield, 2014.

Rogers, Jack. *Jesus, the Bible, and Homosexuality: Explore the Myths, Heal the Church.* Louisville: Westminster John Knox, 2006.

Ryll, Alexander. "Essential Gay Themed Films to Watch, Making Love." *Gay Essential.* https://en.wikipedia.org/wiki/Making_Love.

Schoenbaum, Hannah. "Report says at least 32 transgender people were killed in the U.S. in 2022." *PBS News Hour,* November 16, 2022. https://www.pbs.org/newshour/nation/report-says-at-least-32-transgender-people-were-killed-in-the-u-s-in-2022.

Sears, James Thomas. *Rebels, Rubyfruit, and Rhinestones: Queering Space in the Stonewall South.* New Brunswick, NJ: Rutgers University Press, 2001.

Smith, Christine Marie, ed. *Preaching Justice: Ethnic and Cultural Perspectives.* Eugene, OR: Wipf and Stock, 2008.

"Statement of Faith." Gloria Dei Church of Huntingdon Valley, PA. https://gloriadei.com/who-we-are/.

The Trevor Project. "Top-line Statistics." https://www.thetrevorproject.org/resources/article/facts-about-lgbtq-youth-suicide/.

Viefhues-Bailey, Ludger H. "Religious Interests Between Bible and Politics." In *Between a Man and a Woman? Why Conservatives Oppose Same-Sex Marriage,* 29–60. New York: Columbia University Press, 2010. http://www.jstor.org/stable/10.7312/vief15620.6.

Wiseman, Karyn L. "A 'Sexegetical' Theory for Preparing to Preach on Human Sexuality." Paper presented to the Ethics in Preaching section of the Academy of Homiletics, December 4, 2013.

——— "Writing for the Ear." In *Writing Theologically: Foundations for Learning,* edited by Eric D. Barreto, 33–43. Minneapolis: Fortress, 2015.

"What is HIV?" Center for Disease Control. https://www.cdc.gov/hiv/basics/whatishiv.html.

"Why It Took Decades for LGBTQ Stories to Be Included in Holocaust History" *Time* Magazine, April 27, 2021. https://time.com/5953047/lgbtq-holocaust-stories/.

Workin, Joel R. *Dear God, I Am Gay—Thank You!* Chicago: Extraordinary Lutheran Ministries, 2012.

Zive, Gayle. "A Brief History of Western Homosexuality." *Stanislaus State Journal.* https://www.csustan.edu/sites/default/files/honors/documents/journals/sexinstone/Zive.pdf.